הכוזרי

The Kuzari
Part I and II

Rabbi Yehudah Halevi

Translated and Annotated by
Avraham Yaakov Finkel

YESHIVATH BETH MOSHE
SCRANTON, PA.

ISBN 1-892692-03-1

CONTENTS

—◦◉◦—

הקדמה
מהראש ישיבה
מורינו הרב יעקב שניידמאן שליט״א

אך למותר לספר מחשיבות ספר הכוזרי די לנו בזה שנתקבל
בכל תפוצות ישראל בכל הדורות, לספר יסודי בענין השקפות
הנצרכים למאמינים ועובדי הי״ת. אמנם יש לנו לקבל התעוררות
יתירה מהמעשה שעליה נבנה הספר אשר יש הוכחות ברורות שהוא
מעשה שהיה ולא רק משל בעלמא ואף שלא נזכר מעשה נורא כזה
בספרי הסטוריה של אוה״ע הרי ע הרי גם מעשה היטלר ימ״ש עם כלל
ישראל נשמט מהרבה ספרי הסטוריה או שנזכר כלאחר יד בב' או ג'
שורות ולא עוד אלא שהרבה כופרים בו לגמרי.

ומעשה שהיה כך היה: מלך כוזר היה לו חלום פעם אחר פעם
שמלאך ה' הגיד לו שכוונתו רצויה ואין מעשיו רצויין ותתפעם רוחו
עד ששאל מחכמי הגוים איזהו דרך הישר בעבודתו ית' וכשנתברר
לו ששקר דיברו קרא אל חכם א' מחכמי ישראל והתוכח עמו עד
שביאר לו כל יסודות היהדות. כשראה המלך אמיתת דבריו עמד
ונתגייר וגייר כל עמו אתו.

והמעשה נפלאה איך ובמה זכה מלך זה שקרבו הקב״ה
לעבודתו בחלום כזה פעם אחר פעם. ונראה שהוא מקרא מפורש
באיוב פרק לג' פסוק יד' כי באחת ידבר אל וכו' בחלום חזיון לילה
וכו' אז יגלה אזן אנשים ובמסרם יחתם. הרי מבואר שמדבר ה' עם
כל אדם פעמים בחלום ופעמים ע״י מאורעות שונות ומי שיטה אזן
ישמע קולו שמדבר עם כל יחיד ויחיד וכמו שאמר לו המלאך
שכוונתו רצויה. עוד נראה שאותו המלך היה מכלל הבא ליטהר
מסעיין אותו וביקש האמת לאמיתו וכשנתברר לו האמת קיבל עליו
לעזוב את דרכו ולהתגייר עם כל בני עמו.

v

והנה ברכת ה׳ היא תעשיר שלא די שזכה הוא לחסות תחת
כנפי השכינה אלא שבאת ההשפעה גם על כל בני עמו שזכו כולן
להתגייר ואף אנו בני ישראל זכינו על ידי זה שנתגלה בפירסום יסודי
אמונתינו ונכתב מחמת זה המלך ספר הכוזרי המחזיק ידינו בכל
הדורות.

וכן אמרו חז״ל על הפסוק כל השומע יצחק לי הרבה עקרות
נפקדו עמה, הרבה חולים נתרפאו בו ביום, שכשיורדת הברכה
יורדת בשפע וטוב לצדיק וטוב לשכינו.

ואם ככה לגוי שעדיין לא נתגייר לבני ישראל עאכו״כ שתרד
הברכה לזוכין בה בשפע רב על כל גודותיו ויתברכו כל הנלוים עמו.

המקום ישמינו מכלל הבאים ליטהר לשמוע בקול דברו שעי״ז
נזכה לברכה עד בלי די. יתמלא המעיין ויפוץ החוצה.

TRANSLATION OF RABBI YAAKOV
SCHNAIDMAN'S PROLOGUE

<hr />

The Kuzari has been accepted among The Jewish people for generations as a fundamental guide to Torah outlook and philosophy. It is therefore unnecessary to elaborate on the importance of this work.

However, we can point out an additional lesson that can be learnt from the story of the Kuzari king around which this work is based. (Although the story is not found in history books there are clear indications that it did, if fact, take place. This is similar to Hitler's war against the Jews which is often not mentioned in history books. Even the few that do mention it deal with it in a few short lines. In fact, many deny the destruction of European Jewry altogether.)

In the introduction to the Kuzari, Rabbi Yehuda Halevy relates that the king of the Khazars had a recurring dream where an angel told him that his intentions were pleasing to God but not his actions. He was very troubled and decided to ask the wise men of various faiths the true path of God's service. After verifying the falsehood of other faiths, he called a Jewish sage and debated with him until all the fundamentals of Judaism were explained. The king became convinced of the truth of his words and converted along with the rest of his nation.

It is remarkable that the king merited that Hashem spoke to him in a dream and thereby brought him close to Him. This idea is mentioned in the verse *"For God speaks once . . . In a dream at night . . . He uncovers the ears of people and seals them to suffering . . . in order to refrain man from his course of action." (Job 33:14-18)*. We see that Hashem speaks to everyone, at times in a dream and at times through events that occur. One who is attentive will be motivated by this call to return to Hashem.

Also because the king sought the truth he was considered "one who comes to purify himself" who is helped from above.

Not only did the king merit to become close to Hashem, but his whole nation merited along with him. In fact the entire Jewish nation merited through him, because, due to him the fundamentals of our faith were expressly stated and elaborated on.

In a similar vein our Sages said that many barren women gave birth at the time that Sora was blessed with a child. This is because when goodness comes from Hashem it comes in great abundance, and the good given to the righteous is shared with his neighbor.

If this great outpouring of Hashem's love came to a non-Jew, surely the blessing that comes to a Jew who merits it, will be so great as to affect all that surround him.

May the Almighty place us among those that come to purify themselves and hear His words, thereby meriting His unlimited blessing.

TRANSLATOR'S INTRODUCTION

—◉—

The Kuzari, one of the foremost works on Jewish philosophy of all time, is the greatest achievement of Rabbi Yehudah Halevi (1080-1145), the great rabbi, poet and philosopher of the medieval Golden Age of Spanish Jewry. It has influenced the thinking of Jews to the present day.

The framework of the book is based on the conversion to Judaism of a pagan king in the distant empire of the Khazars. In a recurring dream the king was told by an angel, *"Your intentions [of finding God] are pleasing to God, but your actions are not."* Searching for the true religion, the king questioned a Christian scholar, a Moslem sage, and finally, a rabbi. After listening to the arguments of the Christian and Moslem representatives, the king found Judaism to be the true religion. As a result, he and many of his subjects converted to Judaism.

The Kuzari is structured on the rabbi's dialogue with the Khazar king. In a question-and-answer format the rabbi expounds on the fundamentals of Judaism and analyzes a multitude of other facets, ranging from music to the location of the international dateline, from a discussion of the oral tradition to the theme of reward and punishment.

Rabbi Yehudah Halevi's main idea is that God revealed Himself through history, in contrast to the belief of Rabbeinu Saadyah Gaon who holds that Creation *ex nihilo* ["something out of nothing"] is the fundamental tenet of Judaism. And so the rabbi tells the Kuzari king in down-to-earth terms: *"We believe in the God of*

Abraham, Isaac, and Jacob, Who took the Jews out of Egypt with great wonders and miracles. . ." He explains that, *"Israel among the nations is like a heart among the organs."* The Jewish people is the servant of God. Their suffering atones for the sins of the world. It is precisely the miserable condition of the Jew that testifies to his mission. The Torah is real; it was given publicly to the entire Jewish people at Sinai, not just to a few individuals. The Jewish nation, Eretz Yisrael, and Torah are a unity. Eretz Yisrael is superior to any other land, and the Hebrew language is the most important of all languages.

In the Kuzari, Rabbi Yehudah Halevi proves that the Jewish world is based on three fundamentals: 1) Divine revelation, 2) the Jewish people and its language, 3) the observance of the mitzvos. The book has had a major impact on Jewish thought and has inspired successive generations with a burning love for Torah and Eretz Yisrael.

The Kuzari originally written in Arabic around 1140, was translated by R. Yehudah ibn Tibbon and has been reprinted numerous times. Two classical commentaries in the Vilna edition (1914): *Kol Yehudah*, by R.Yehudah Moscato and *Otzar Nechmad*, by R. Yisrael Halevi, were very helpful to me in clarifying the often obscure Hebrew of Ibn Tibbon's literal translation.

The story of the conversion of the Khazar king and his people has fascinated historians. A number of books have been written on the subject, and various theories have been put forward. The Khazar country was destroyed by the Mongols around 1230. The Khazar people were scattered among other nations and lost their ethnic identity.

Today, nine centuries after the Kuzari was written, the book is as relevant as ever. The dialogue format keeps you spellbound, wondering how the rabbi will respond to the challenging questions. In the process, some of your own doubts are resolved and your *emunah* is strengthened immeasurably.

Avraham Yaakov Finkel
Shevat, 5760/2000

THE KUZARI

Part I

———◦◉◦———

INTRODUCTION

1. I[1] was asked what arguments I could offer to refute the philosophies and religious beliefs that speak against our faith, including the tenets of the Karaite sect[2] which are opposed to traditional Judaism.

This brought to mind the arguments advanced by a rabbi[3] who had a dialogue with a Khazar king. From historical records we know that [Kuzari][4] the king, converted to Judaism about four hundred years ago.

The king had a recurring dream in which an angel appeared to him nightly, saying, "Your intentions [of finding God] are pleasing to the Creator, but your actions are not." The king was a devout follower of the Khazar religion, so much so, that he personally conducted the Khazar temple services and offered their sacrifices in the sincere belief that God wanted this of him. But no matter how hard

---

[1]   Rabbi Yehudah Halevi.

[2]   The Karaites were a Jewish sect that observed only those mitzvos that are mentioned in the Written Torah, refusing to accept the interpretations of the Oral Torah given to Moshe and transmitted by the Sages of the Mishnah and Gemara.

[3]   Rabbi Yitzchak HaSangari. According to *Seder Hadoros* his name was Rabbi Yitzchak Almangari.

[4]   The king's name was Bulan, but in this work he is identified as Kuzari.

1

he tried to serve God, the angel returned each night and repeated, "Your intentions are pleasing to God, but not your actions."

This prompted the king to explore other beliefs and religions. [In his search for the true faith he questioned a philosopher, a Christian scholar, a Moslem teacher, and a rabbi]. The rabbi's rational arguments made sense to him and gave him inner peace, therefore he and large numbers of his subjects converted to Judaism.

To address the questions at hand I decided to record the dialogue between the Kuzari and the rabbi. Thus the subject matter will be presented in a format that is easy to follow and understand.

DIALOGUE WITH OTHER FAITHS

When the king dreamed that God approved of his intentions but not his actions, he assumed that God wanted him to find for himself the way of life God favors. He began his research by questioning the foremost philosopher of his time about his religious beliefs.

The Philosopher Speaks

[Translator's note: It should be pointed out that the Aristotelian beliefs advocated by the philosopher which were widely accepted and studied in the medieval period are erroneous, and will be proven false later in this discourse.]

The philosopher explained:

"God does not favor or dislike anything. He is way above such concepts as wishing or deploring. When one wishes for something, he is lacking that which he hopes to gain. He feels satisfied only once he reaches his goal. [But since God is perfect and lacks nothing, He cannot desire or want anything.]

"What's more, philosophers believe that God is far too exalted to know the trivial details of this world. This must be so, because whatever happens in this physical world is forever changing, whereas God is not physical, and therefore His knowledge never changes. Therefore, God does not know you, much less your thoughts and actions. And surely, He does not listen to your prayers or watch what you are doing.

"When philosophers say that God created you, they mean it in a figurative sense. What they are suggesting is that God is the Prime Cause of all that exists, [and all of creation evolved from this Prime Cause], but God did not intentionally create you. God never created man. The universe has always existed, it has no beginning. Man has always existed. No man came into being other than through a father who lived before him; each generation, was fathered by the generation before it.

"A human being possesses spiritual powers, feelings [like light-heartedness or depression], and character traits [like humility, anger, haughtiness] which he inherited from his parents and other relatives. External conditions also affect a person's individuality: factors like climate, the region on earth where he lives, diet, the quality of his food and water, celestial spheres, the constellations of the zodiac, stars and planets; all these influence his personality.

"Everything that happens in the universe can be traced back to a First Cause.[5] That does not mean that the First Cause planned it. Rather the First Cause set into motion a second cause which in turn produced a third and fourth cause, and so on. These causes and their effects unfolded from the First Cause in an uninterrupted chain down to nature as we know it.

"In nature no two things are exactly alike; they vary depending on the elements they are made of and the environmental influences affecting them. Some things with an ideal mix of elements will be perfect, others, with a flawed blend of elements will be imperfect. An example of an imperfect human would be a Cushite. To be sure,

---

5   Each event was caused by something that preceded it: Rain makes grass grow, clouds produce rain, water rising from the oceans causes clouds to form. The water of the oceans is made of atoms. But what are atoms made of? No series of causes can run on forever. Sooner or later we come to an end for which we know no reason: a supreme and final end for the sake of which everything else exists, the Prime Cause.

a Cushite is a member of the human race, but, due to the extremely hot climate of his region, he cannot think straight or express himself clearly. On the other hand, when it comes to the philosopher, the outside influences that work on his personality are perfectly balanced. As a result, he can reach the peak in character traits, intelligence, and good deeds; he lacks nothing to make him perfect.

"Understand that these abilities are only potential abilities that lie dormant within him. The philosopher must bring them to reality through study and self-discipline. When he does that, he will achieve his full capacity of becoming a perfect human being. There are an infinite number of stages between the Cushite on the one hand and the philosopher on the other.

"Such an ideal human being will perceive a divine light, called the Active Intellect that will eliminate all worldly tendencies in him. When a person's intellect is illuminated by the Active Intellect he will attach himself to this light to the point where there will be no difference between the person and the Active Intellect. He will have stripped himself of all physical desires and aspirations. At this point, all his limbs and organs will strive to do only the most perfect deeds, at the most appropriate time, and under optimal conditions. Since this person's intellect has been freed from worldly interests, it is as though his mind has become a tool in the service of the Active Intellect. Before he was illuminated by the Active Intellect, he would waver between doing good and sinning—now he will do only good. This stage is the highest level of perfection you can hope to attain. When you reach this level, your soul, having been cleansed, will grasp the intrinsic truths of all branches of science. As a result, all your doubts will vanish. Your soul will become like an angel—not just figuratively, but in a real sense—because, like an angel, your soul becomes close to the Active Intellect and detached from physical desires. Like a low-ranking angel, a spiritual being without corporeality, your soul will live on. It is a source of comfort to know that you will be in the company of Hermes, Asclepius, Plato, and Aristotle. You and everyone else who reaches that level of closeness to the Active Intellect become one everlasting union.

'Becoming close' to the Creator, as you put it, is only a figure of speech. The ideal way to become 'close' to God is to study philosophy and abstract thought to the point where your mind advances from passive thinking, [absorbing the knowledge of others] to active, creative thinking.

"Attach yourself to the ways of the righteous, copying their character traits and their deeds. These qualities will help you discover the truth and become like the Active Intellect. If you do so, you will acquire contentment, humility, submissiveness, and every other noble quality. At the same time, you will be paying homage to the First Cause, not for reward, or fear of punishment. Your sole objective will be to unite with the Active Intellect, thereby recognizing the truth and being able to describe things as they really are, for these are the characteristics of the Active Intellect.

"Once you have adopted this way of thinking, don't worry about which theology, formal religion, or rituals to follow, or with what liturgy and language to pray. If you like, you may even make up your own religion, and invent a creed that teaches people to be humble, exalt and praise the Prime Cause, and conduct themselves properly. Do the same for your family and countrymen, if you can get them to listen to you. Or, embrace as your religion the rational set of rules the philosophers have developed, and strive for purity of soul, so that you will gain a clear understanding of all there is to know.

"To sum it up: Try to gain a pure heart through any religion that appeals to you, as long as you have a clear understanding of the essence of wisdom. Doing that, you will reach your goal, getting close to this intangible being, the Active Intellect. It may very well be that the Active Intellect will give you prophetic insight and reveal to you future events in true dreams and visions."

The Kuzari Takes Issue With the Philosopher

2. The Kuzari: "Your explanation makes sense, but it does not answer my question. [You said that God is not aware of man's ac-

tions, and that all that matters is to search for the truth, purify your soul, and acquire good character traits.] I am sure that my soul is pure, and that my actions are intended to please the Creator. Nevertheless, the message I am getting in my dreams is, that although my intentions are good, my actions are not pleasing to God. Clearly, there must be a way of acting that is desirable in and of itself, and not just as a means to improve one's thinking process, as you seem to think.

"If this were not so, [that there is a way of acting that is inherently desirable to God,] how do you explain that *Edom* and *Yishmael* [i.e., Christianity and Islam], two religions that divide the civilized world between them, are constantly fighting because of their religious differences. Each of them is serving his God with pure intention; among them there are monks and hermits who follow an ascetic life style of fasting and praying, and yet they still kill each other. To make things worse, they believe that their killing is commendable and a means of getting closer to God. Each side believes his way leads to the Garden of Eden. [The fact that both sides are willing to sacrifice their lives for their religious beliefs proves that they believe there is a set of actions that is inherently pleasing to God.] And don't tell me to follow the tenets of both religions. Believing in two conflicting faiths is absurd, [but since both sides agree, that there exists a set of actions that is inherently pleasing to God, that seems to be a reasonable idea]."

3. The philosopher: "The philosophers's religion does not condone killing, [and to us a holy war makes no sense.] The primary aim of our creed is to achieve clearheaded thinking."

4. The Kuzari: "[Is the only objection you philosophers have against the two religions that they act irrationally by fighting religious wars?] Don't you disagree also with their belief that the world had a beginning, that it was created in six days, and that [what you call] the Prime Cause actually speaks to human beings who are worthy of prophecy. Doesn't all this contradict the philosophers' view that the Prime Cause is above knowing worldly things?

"[If what you say is true, that philosophers are like angels and similar to the Active Intellect,] then, given their way of life, their wisdom, and their search for the truth, we might expect many of them to be prophets. In fact, by now we should have heard reports of great miracles they performed; they should have become famous celebrities. Yet we see just the opposite: people who have not studied science or delved into philosophy have had true visions, whereas philosophers and scientists have not received any heavenly messages. This proves that the right approach to God lies along a different route; not the one you, the philosopher, have suggested."

Dialogue With The Christian Cleric

[Since the philosopher's answer was unacceptable,] the Kuzari said to himself: "Let me go and ask Edom [the Christians] and Yishmael [the Moslems]. Surely, one of these religions must please God. There is no need to investigate the Jewish religion. The fact that the Jews are small in number and everyone despises them tells me that their religion must be untrue."

The Kuzari invited a Christian cleric and asked him about his religion. The Christian said:

"I believe that the universe was created [and has a beginning], and that the Creator, blessed be He, preceded every being that was created. He created the whole world in six days, and all mankind descends from Adam. God oversees all of creation and pays close attention to the actions of man. He shows anger [to sinners] and has compassion [for the righteous]. He speaks, appears, and reveals Himself to His prophets and devout ones and dwells among those whose actions please Him. All that is written in the Torah and the Books of the Jews is true. There can be no doubt about the authenticity of their Scriptures, because the miracles described in them were witnessed by the multitudes of the nations of the world, [not just by a few individuals]."

[Translator's note: In an older edition of the Kuzari the cleric goes on to expound on the Christian doctrine of the virgin birth of the Nazarene, their so-called "savior," on his death on the cross, on the trinity, and the twelve apostles. This is omitted in the classic Vilna edition of 1914.]

5. The Kuzari: "There is no logic to your reasoning; if anything, logic tells me the exact opposite. If you observe something with your own eyes, you cannot help but believe what you are seeing, even if you do not understand it. You then must adapt your logic to what you saw and find a reasonable explanation for the facts you now know. This is the scientific method of research. When a scientist observes a phenomenon he cannot understand, he tries to find a logical explanation for it. When he hears a report of an event that does not agree with his preconceived theory, he rejects the report. But when you demonstrate through an experiment that it is so, he revises his theory and finds a way to explain the phenomenon. After all, you cannot deny what your eyes are seeing.

"As far as I am concerned, I have no evidence that what you say is true. In fact, it sounds quite farfetched. I was not brought up in your religion and was not indoctrinated in these dogmas. I must take a close look at other faiths in my search for the truth."

Dialogue with the Moslem Mullah

Next the Kuzari invited a Moslem mullah and questioned him about his beliefs and rituals.

The Moslem said: "We firmly believe in the Oneness and eternity of God, that the world was created by God, and that all men descended from Adam, the first man. We reject the notion that God has physical qualities. If you find any mention of physical attributes of God in [the Koran], our Scripture, we explain that these passages were written in a figurative sense, to help us understand esoteric concepts. We also believe that our holy book is the word of God. In fact, its marvelous imagery and sublime metaphors are proof of this. No human being could ever compose a book to match its beauty, not even a single verse of it.

We believe that [Mohammed] our prophet is the last of the prophets. He nullified all teachings that came before him and directs all nations to embrace Islam. The reward [in the hereafter] of one who converts to Islam is the return of his soul to his body in the Garden of Eden. There he will enjoy pure delight, given anything he desires and never lacking food, drink, or women. But those that defy the prophet's teachings will go down into the never-ending fire of Gehinnom, to suffer everlasting pain."

6. The Kuzari: "If you want to convince a non believer that God exists and speaks to mortal man, begin by telling him about great miracles that cannot be denied. If he then believes in a Creator,] you still have to convince him that God has spoken to man. You say that the Koran is a marvel of incomparable poetic beauty, which proves the existence of God. That may be so, but the Koran is written in Arabic, and someone like me who does not speak Arabic cannot appreciate its exquisite beauty. And were you to read the Koran to me all day long, I could not tell the difference between it and any other Arabic book. [So, to me, the Koran does not prove that Islam is the true faith.]"

7. The Moslem: "Our prophet did perform miracles, [but we have no record of them. If you want proof, learn Arabic, and you will find the truth you are looking for in the Koran.] We believe that Islam needs no proof by miracles. [It is based on rational thought, and nothing in it contradicts reason.]"

Miracles Witnessed by the Masses

8. The Kuzari: "I believe that the Creator [Who is a spiritual Being] would only communicate with a man of flesh and blood, accompanied by a supernatural event. Thus the person receiving the

Divine message would be certain that the Creator of the world was speaking to him. Furthermore, the supernatural event must take place in full view of multitudes, who see it with their own eyes, not having to rely on tales, legends, and traditions handed down to them over the ages. Having witnessed the miraculous event, they could believe the prophet's message without a shadow of a doubt and without wondering whether it was the result of hallucination or black magic. Only if a miracle occurs, can we hope that people will accept this momentous concept—that the Creator of this world and the next, of the angels, the heavens, the sun, moon, and stars, relates to a wretched earthly creature, such as man, speaking to him, and fulfilling his wishes.

Moslems Believe the Miracles of the Torah

9. The Moslem: "But our Koran is full of the stories of Moshe and the children of Israel. No one denies that God punished Pharaoh, that He parted the Red Sea to save His chosen people, and drowned those that angered Him. No one questions the fact that God sent the manna and the quail to feed the children of Israel in the wilderness for forty years; that He spoke to Moshe on Mount Sinai; that He made the sun stand still for Joshua, and that He helped Joshua defeat the Anakim, the mighty giants of the land of Canaan. Let us also not forget what God did before the Jewish nation appeared on the scene. I am referring to the Flood and the destruction of Sodom and Amorah. Everyone knows that these things happened. No one suggests that these miracles are deceptions or illusions."

DIALOGUE WITH THE RABBI

10. [Regretting that he dismissed Judaism as unworthy of consideration,] the Kuzari said: "I realize now that I have to ask the Jews. All religions agree that they are the offspring of the children of

Israel. The Jews are living proof that God's Torah is the foundation of the world." He invited [Rabbi Yitzchak HaSangari], a rabbi, and asked him about his faith.

11. The Rabbi: "We believe in the God of Avraham, Yitzchok, and Yaakov, Who took the children of Israel out of Egypt with great signs and wonders. He fed them in the wilderness and gave them the land of Canaan after having led them across the Red Sea and the Jordan River with great miracles. This God sent Moshe [to the people] to give them His Torah. In the course of time, He sent thousands of prophets who admonished the people to observe the Torah, assuring a rich reward for those who keep the Torah and harsh punishment for the disobedient.

"We believe everything that is written in the Torah, which includes a vast body of knowledge."

12. The Kuzari: "Originally I decided to omit asking the Jews about their religion, assuming that since they lost their past glory, they lacked insight and wisdom. I thought that due to misery and poverty they were devoid of any noble quality. [Now that I heard your answer, I realize that I was right in my negative assessment. Since the Jews have taught the world to believe in the Creator and His close supervision over each person,] you, Jew, should have answered me that you believe in the Creator of the world, Who oversees and guides the universe, and Who created and sustains you. You should have brought forward these and other universal ideas that are accepted by all religions. It is because of these lofty principles that a believer searches for the truth and strives to model himself after the Creator in His righteousness and wisdom, [and not because of the miracles of the past you cited]."

13. The Rabbi: "You are speaking of a religion that is based on philosophical analysis and reflection. But this type of reasoning leads to great uncertainty. Thus when you ask philosophers about their beliefs you will find that they don't agree on any mode of conduct or on any fundamental principle. This is because philosophers arrive at their conclusions through theoretical speculation. Some of their theories can be substantiated by established facts, others [are not proven but] seem reasonable, and sometimes they offer theories that are not even plausible, much less verifiable by actual facts. [Therefore I opened my remarks by mentioning documented historical facts on which the Jewish religion is based.]"

14. The Kuzari: "I see what you mean. But what you say now is more to the point than your opening statement. Please, continue."

15. The Rabbi: "On the contrary! My opening remarks are of pivotal importance. They are the conclusive proof to my religion. What's more, it is a proof that is self-evident and needs no supporting arguments."

16. The Kuzari: "How so?"

17. The Rabbi: "Allow me to make a few preliminary comments, because I have a feeling that you find my words hard to swallow."

18. The Kuzari: "Let me hear what you have to say."

19. The Rabbi: "Suppose you were told that the king of India is a benevolent man, worthy of praise and honor. As proof of this you were told that his subjects are righteous and virtuous people who deal fairly with each other. Would this be sufficient grounds for you to believe in and praise the king?"

20. The Kuzari: "Why should I? Maybe the Indian people are righteous by nature. They may not even have a king. Then again, they may be righteous because of their king. Or it may just be that both the king and his people are inherently righteous."

21. The Rabbi: "Now, suppose the king's messengers bring you gifts from India. You are absolutely sure that these gifts could have come only from the king's palace. Accompanying the gifts there is a letter in the king's own handwriting, bearing the royal seal. Along with the gifts and the letter there are medicines to cure your sicknesses and preserve your health. The package contains also poisons to be used against your enemies. With these poisonous weapons you can destroy your enemy without firing a shot. Wouldn't you feel that out of gratitude you have to abide by the king's wishes and pay homage to him?"

22. The Kuzari: Yes, I certainly would. To begin with, [the king's letter and his gifts] would settle my doubt as to whether the people of India indeed had a king. I also would be convinced that the king knows me and wants to do favors for me."

23. The Rabbi: "If someone were to ask you what you think of this king, what would you say?"

24. The Kuzari: "I would start by mentioning the things for which I have tangible evidence, namely the gifts. Then I would add that through the marvelous gifts he sent I could tell what a great king he is."

25. The Rabbi: "This is exactly the way I answered you when you first posed your question. Moshe also spoke this way to Pharaoh when he told him, 'the God of the Hebrews sent me', implying, the God of Avraham, Yitzchok and Yaakov. He referred to the God of the Patriarchs because the nations of the time knew that God spoke to the Patriarchs, guiding them, and performing miracles for them. Notice that Moshe did not say, 'the God of heaven and earth has sent me to you,' or, 'my Creator and your Creator sent me.'

"Likewise, when God spoke to the Jewish people at Mount Sinai, He began, '*I am God, your Lord, Who has taken you out of the land of Egypt (Shemos 20:2),* God did not introduce Himself by saying, 'I am the Creator of the universe and your Creator.'

"When you asked me about my religion, I answered the same way Moshe did. I told you what I and all the Jewish people are required to believe, having seen with our own eyes that God gave the

Torah at Mount Sinai. The report of this overwhelming event was handed down in an uninterrupted chain from generation to generation, so that it is just as if we ourselves had been present at the Giving of the Torah."

26. The Kuzari: "If this is so, it seems to me that your Torah was given to no one but you, the Jewish people, and no other nation is required to keep it."

27. The Rabbi: "Quite right; non-Jews do not have to observe the Torah. However, although the Torah is the exclusive heritage of the Jews, any non-Jew who joins our people will share whatever good God grants us, just not to the same degree [with regard to inheriting a share of Eretz Yisrael]. If the obligation to keep the Torah were based on the fact that God created us, then all mankind—white and black alike—would have to observe the Torah, for God created them all. The fact is that only we Jews have the duty to live by the Torah, because God took us out of Egypt, and bound His glory to us. He chose us because we are the treasured of all people."

28. The Kuzari: "Hold it, Jew! You are beginning to sing a different tune now. Your speech has turned sour after starting out so sweet.[6]"

29. The Rabbi: "Sour or sweet—just pay attention, and let me explain."

30. The Kuzari: "Go ahead; say what's on your mind."

30. The Rabbi: "When you look at nature, you find that every living creature needs nourishment, grows, reproduces, and has specific biological functions. This is the case with plants and animals, but not with inorganic matter like earth, stones, metals, and the elements."

---

6   The Kuzari became angry hearing that there existed a chosen people with whom the Creator had a special relationship, and that this was the pathetic Jewish nation.

32. The Kuzari: "You are making a sweeping statement that needs clarification, although basically, it is true."

33. The Rabbi: "When it comes to living organisms we can say that animals are superior to plant life in that they have a life force that gives them mobility, instincts, behavioral traits, senses, memory, desires, and the like."

34. The Kuzari: "That's obviously true; no one can deny it."

35. The Rabbi: "When it comes to intellect, we agree that it was granted to man alone, and this sets him apart from the animal kingdom. The intellect calls on man to observe the rules of morality, obey the laws of his city and country, and live by the accepted norms and customs."

36. The Kuzari: "That is also true."

37. The Rabbi: "And what level do you think is above that of man?"

38. The Kuzari: "The level of the great sages."

39. The Rabbi: "I am talking about differences between things that are in separate categories, like the difference between plants and minerals, or man and animal. Classifying people or things that are in the same grouping, separating them according to who has more wisdom and who has less, is useless. Such differences do not change the nature of a thing, [a wise or ignorant person, is still a member of the human race]."

40. The Kuzari: "If so, [that you draw the line only between man and beast], then there is no living creature on a higher level than man."

41. The Rabbi: "But suppose we found a man who walked through fire unharmed, went without food and did not starve and whose face radiated a glow so dazzling that the eye was blinded by it. He never became sick or frail, and when he reached the end of his days, died willingly at a fixed time, like someone going to bed and falling asleep. Furthermore, he knew everything that happened since the beginning of the world, and everything that will happen until the end of time. Wouldn't you agree that this person is unique and in a class by himself?"

42. The Kuzari: "A person like that would be Divine being, like an angel, if he existed at all. He would be in the godly class, not a member of the human, animal or organic realm."

43. The Rabbi: "What I mentioned are just a few of the qualities of our prophet [Moshe. We know that he was not harmed by the fire in which God descended on Mount Sinai and he did not eat or drink for forty days while he was on Mount Sinai to receive the Torah.] All major religions agree on this point. It was through Moshe that God revealed Himself to the Jewish people [at Mount Sinai], and it was through him that they recognized that they have a God Who guides them according to His will and repays them according to the way they behave. Moshe told the Jews things they never knew, like how the world was created and what happened to mankind before the great Flood. He told them about the generations that linked them to Adam, what transpired during the Flood, and how the seventy nations of the world descended from Shem, Cham and Yefet, the sons of Noach. He told them how the seventy languages of the world came into being [when God confused the peoples' language], where the different nations settled, how the different trades and crafts originated, and the chronology from Adam up to this day."

CHRONOLOGY SINCE CREATION

44. The Kuzari: "Amazing, that you should have an exact chronology dating all the way back to Creation!"

45. The Rabbi: "In fact, our calendar is based on this chronology. [Some Jews may have different customs than others,] but the Jewish calendar is one thing all Jews agree on, no matter where they live or where they come from."

46. The Kuzari: "And what year is it now according to your tradition?"

47. The Rabbi: "We are now in the year 4500 [from Creation].[7] The particulars are outlined in our Torah, which lists the lives of Adam, Seth, Enoch down to Noach, then Shem and Ever, to Avraham, Yitzchok and Yaakov, and on to Moshe. These men were the elite and the nobility of their generation. Though they had many children, most of them resembled their fathers only outwardly, lacking their fathers' Divine fervor. The Torah listed only the Divinely inspired men, who were lone individuals in each generation. This continued until Yaakov fathered the twelve tribes, who were all bearers of the message that God created the world and guides it, and oversees the actions of each individual. While before this, the belief in God rested with single individuals, now the story of Creation became the heritage of an entire nation. We, in turn, received this historical record from Moshe and we know how many years elapsed from Moshe to the present [so that we know for a fact that this year is 4500 from Creation]."

48. The Kuzari: "The chronicle of the genealogies in your Torah removes any suspicion of distortion or conspiracy to falsify historical data. It would be impossible for even ten people [to forge the number of years since Creation] without their scheme falling apart. Sooner or later their trickery would come to light. Were anyone to challenge their false chronology they would be unable to contradict him. If ten people could not perpetrate such a hoax, surely an entire generation could not connive to fabricate a bogus date for the

---

7   This corresponds to the year 740 C.E.

creation of the world. Furthermore, the period elapsing between Creation and the Giving of the Torah is too short for any lie to be perpetuated.⁸"

49. The Rabbi: "Quite right. Avraham himself lived during the Generation of the Dispersion [i.e., the generation that built the Tower of Babel]. He and his family retained the [Hebrew] language of his grandfather Ever, and that's why he is called *Avraham haIvri* [i.e., Avraham, descendant of Ever].

"Moshe lived four hundred years later, during a period when science and astronomy flourished. Living in this intellectually advanced society, Moshe approached Pharaoh and the Egyptian scientists [and performed signs and wonders]. Even the Jewish elders at that time looked critically at him, not fully convinced that the Creator would speak with man. Only when they heard God giving them the Ten Commandments did they truly believe in God and His servant Moshe.

"Can you imagine that the Jews of that time could be duped into believing that just five hundred years earlier the only language spoken was Hebrew, and that suddenly in Peleg's time, in Babylonia, the seventy languages sprang up out of the blue in one day—and that nation A descended from [Noach's son] Yefes, nation B from Shem, and nation C from Cham; and that these nations lived in such-and-such countries? Is it possible that someone today could concoct lies about well-known nations, telling us things about their past and languages that happened less than five hundred years ago?"

50. The Kuzari: "You are right. That would be impossible. After all, we have books that were written five hundred years ago. No lie could be spread about a nation's lineage, language, and history, without it being exposed as a fabrication."

51. The Rabbi: "Correct. [If there was no way to substantiate Moshe's claims], why did no one contradict his statements? The

---

8   The Torah was given 2448 years after Creation, and only 792 after the Flood.

Jews themselves would have disputed his claims, not to mention the other nations!"

52. The Kuzari: "Your words are powerful and convincing."

The Hebrew Language, the Seven-Day Week and the Decimal System

53. The Rabbi: "[Let me prove it to you from a different angle.] Do you believe that the world's languages have always existed?"

54. The Kuzari: "No, I don't. All languages began at some point in time when people came to agreement about their vocabularies. You can tell that this is so, because every language [has the same basic forms and] is made up of nouns, verbs, and pronouns. Each word is formed of letters that represent the voice modified by the organs of speech, [not made of grunts and single syllables.]"

55. The Rabbi: "[You claim that people reached an agreement about their language.] Have you ever seen or heard of a nation that [abandoned their original language and] invented a new one?"

56. The Kuzari: "No, I haven't. [That would be highly impractical; for example, all books would have to be rewritten.] No doubt, languages came into being at some point in time, before which none of the languages we know of today existed. I imagine everyone spoke the same language, [Hebrew, the holy tongue that Adam spoke]."

57. The Rabbi: "That's not all. Have you ever heard of a nation that does not accept the conventional seven-day week that starts on Sunday and ends on Saturday? Is it conceivable that all nations from the far east to the west should agree on a seven-day week unless one individual instituted it, or a gathering of the world reached an agreement on this issue?"

58. The Kuzari: "You are right. This could have happened only if all the nations of the world unanimously adopted such a resolution. That is hard to believe. We must say that all men are descendants from one person, either Adam or Noach or someone else, in which case all people of the world received the concept of a seven-day week from a common ancestor."

59. The Rabbi: "That's exactly what I was driving at. But there's more: Take the fact that the entire world agrees on the decimal system. Why would they all settle on the same numeric system, unless they all received this as a tradition from one man."

60. The Kuzari: "How can you maintain that the world [is only 4500 years old] in light of reports that in India there are palaces and temples that supposedly are hundreds of thousands of years old?"

61. The Rabbi: "It would indeed weaken my belief if this report came from a civilized nation, or was found in a universally accepted book whose data is not disputed. But that is not the case with India. They are an uncivilized people whose facts and figures are unreliable. The things they say are meant to corroborate their spurious religion [and their false belief that the world had no beginning]. They provoke other religions with their images, idols, and incantations that they claim are effective. They ridicule anyone who says that he has a book written by God. They themselves have only a few books written by a few pseudo-scholars. Only the dimwitted will be misled by some of their books on astrology in which they speak of things that happened tens of thousands of years ago or by their books called *The Nabatean Agriculture*.[9] This work mentions the names Yanbushar, Sangrit, and Roanai who supposedly lived before Adam. They go so far as to claim Yanbushar was Adam's teacher, and other such nonsense."

62. The Kuzari: "Your answer is convincing, only because I asked

---

[9]   The Rambam debunks this book in his *Moreh Nevuchim*, Part 3, chapter 29. There, he says that it was written by the Sabeans, the religion in which Abraham was raised.

you about the claims of a savage nation that cannot agree on a common belief. But what do you say about the Greek philosophers? They are famous for their analytical research and their relentless probing for the truth. All of them agree that the world is without a beginning. They do not say that the universe existed tens of thousands or millions of years, but that it is infinite, without beginning or end."

63. The Rabbi: "You cannot blame the Greek philosophers for their mistaken views. After all, the Greeks do not have an oral tradition of Divine wisdom, and they never witnessed the Giving of the Torah. The Greeks—descendants of Yefet—live in the northern regions [an area not suited for Divine inspiration; only Eretz Yisrael, the area settled by the descendants of Shem, is adapted to receiving God's word.] The Divinely inspired wisdom, which came down from Adam to Noach, remained only with the offspring of Shem, who was the best of Noach's sons. It has been handed down to us, the treasured nation, in an unbroken and never-ending chain.

"The Greeks acquired their wisdom only after they conquered the Persian empire and adopted its wisdom. Persia, in turn, acquired their wisdom from the Babylonians [when King Cyrus of Persia conquered Babylonia. The Babylonians acquired their wisdom from the Jewish captives they brought to their country after the destruction of the first Beis Hamikdash]. It was only at that point in time—not before and not after—that the famous Greek philosophers appeared on the scene. Ever since the Roman empire supplanted the Greek kingdom, the Greeks have produced no philosopher worth mentioning. [This proves that their wisdom was borrowed from the Jews. If the Greeks had innate wisdom, there would be leading Greek philosophers and scholars to this day.]"

Rejection of Aristotle's Philosophy

64. The Kuzari: "Just because the great Aristotle did not receive the tradition of Creation from Shem, his principles should be discarded? [After all, he did offer analytical proof in support of his theory of the timelessness of the universe.]"

65. The Rabbi: "Aristotle's doctrine should be dismissed. Aristotle strained his mind [probing the secrets of the universe] because he had no reliable tradition to follow. He pondered about how the world began, and how it would eventually end. It was just as hard for him to comprehend that the world had a beginning as it was to conceive of a world that had no beginning and always existed. In the end, his analysis led him to the conclusion that the universe is timeless; without beginning or end. It never occurred to him to research the books of earlier generations that dealt with Creation; the age of the world; and how mankind descended from the three sons of Noach. Had Aristotle lived among the [Jewish] nation which had a well-documented and undisputed tradition, he would have applied himself to finding proofs for the idea that the universe was created—as perplexing as it is—instead of arguing for the concept of a universe without beginning, which is even more baffling."

66. The Kuzari: [Thinking that Aristotle had offered positive proof for the eternity of the universe, the Kuzari asks:] "How can you contradict something that has already been proven?"

67. The Rabbi: "Who says he proved it? God forbid! The Torah does not expect us to believe something that goes against proven facts. The Torah does tell us, however, about miracles and changes in the laws of nature, [like water changing into blood, or a rod into a snake], in order to teach us about God's wisdom and His ability to do whatever He wants, whenever He decides to do so.

"[However, there is no proof for the notion that the world has always existed, as you seem to think.] Whether the universe was created or is eternal is a profound question, and a case can be made for either view. The factor that weighs in favor of Creation is the tradition that dates back from Adam to Noach and down to the prophecies of Moshe. These are certainly more trustworthy than philosophical speculation.

"If a Jew who believes in the Torah thinks that the world was created from primeval matter,[10] and that many worlds, made from the same primeval matter existed before this one, this would not be considered a flaw in his faith. For he still would believe that this world was created at a given point in time, and that all mankind descended from Adam and Eve."

68. The Kuzari: "So far I am quite happy with your arguments on this subject. If we continue our friendship, I will eventually ask you for more positive proofs. But, how can you believe that the Creator of matter, life, intellect, souls, and angels, Who is so exalted, holy, and great beyond the grasp of angels, let alone, of the human senses, has contact with [man] a creature made of lowly and despicable physicality. Granted, that the human being is a marvelous creation, but even the anatomy of the lowly tiny insect manifests a wisdom that is way beyond human understanding."

WHAT IS NATURE?

69. The Rabbi: "I can answer that in just a few short sentences. Do you ascribe the wisdom you detect in the anatomy of an ant to the influence of a star, a galaxy or something other than God Almighty, Who weighs and measures everything with absolute precision?"

70. The Kuzari: "The anatomy of an ant is nature's doing."

71. The Rabbi: "And what do you mean by 'nature'"?

72. The Kuzari: "The scientists call it a kind of force. I admit, I don't have the foggiest idea what they mean by that, but I'm sure the scientists know what they are talking about."

---

[10] This is one of the principles of Plato's philosophy. Plato believed that the universe was created from a primeval clot of matter called *hiyuli*.

73. The Rabbi: "Believe me, they don't know any more than we do. Aristotle vaguely defined nature as the primary cause that makes things move or rest, as long as these changes are inherent—not incidental—to these things."[11]

74. The Kuzari: "Aristotle seems to be saying that an object that changes inherently—in and of itself—[like a plant that grows or dies]—has a cause that makes it change. He calls that cause "nature.""

75. The Rabbi: "Aristotle drew a sharp distinction between things that move or rest accidentally [through outside influences] and things that move or rest inherently, by nature."

76. The Kuzari: "If so, [that nature is the cause that makes things grow,] I realize that these thinkers have misled us with the definition of the word "nature." They have us believe that nature has the power to think and act, just as God does. Why don't we just say 'God' instead of 'nature'?"

77. The Rabbi: "You are right. When we speak of 'the wisdom of nature' we mean the wisdom of the Creator. Still, the term 'nature' should not be cast aside completely; it does have some validity. The sun, moon, and stars, all have inherent powers, such as warming, cooling, providing moisture and dryness. They do these things, not because they have a will and can think on their own, but because God appointed them to perform these functions. However, the composition of all living things, their ability to reproduce, and their will can be attributed only to the All-knowing, Almighty God. You may you use the term 'nature' to describe the functions of the sun, moon, and the planets which affect the climate of the world, as long as you don't credit them with any intelligence. A man and woman who have a child did not actually create and form the baby.

---

11 "Inherent change" refers to: birth, growth, wilting, death and decay. "Incidental change" refers to outside influences that bring about change.

They only supplied the seed which is the raw material which is shaped by the Creator into the human form.

"Do not harbor any doubt that God's influence on this lowly physical world touches and forms every species to the extent that it is capable of receiving that influence. This concept is the root of faith, and also the root of disbelief."

78. The Kuzari: "How can the root of faith at the same time be the root of disbelief?"

Torah Leads to Godliness

79. The Rabbi: "Let me explain. The conditions that cause the Divine Presence to descend are beyond human understanding. For example, we know that sacrifices cause the *Shechina*—Hashem's Glory—to come down to the world. But we do not know how many sacrifices we should offer, what animals to offer, where, how and when to offer them. Special detailed instructions from God are necessary to know the laws of the offerings. Whoever acquires this knowledge and follows the instructions meticulously and whole-heartedly is a believer. But if someone tries to cause the *Shechinah* to descend [by designing temples and inventing altar services] on the basis of intellectual analysis, deductions and inferences, or by applying the things he finds in books on astrology and occultism, such a person is a non-believer. Such a person will bring sacrifices and burn incense based on his own rational deductions, but he actually has no idea what he should be doing—how much he should offer, where, when, with whom, and how he should offer, and so on.

"A person trying to reach closeness to God through intellectual probing is like a fool entering the office of a doctor famous for the medicines he dispenses. The doctor is not in, but people come for their medications. The fool hands out pills and potions from the doctor's medicine cabinet without knowing what medicine to give, in what dosage, and for what sickness. He ends up killing many people with the very medicines that were meant to cure them. If by chance, one person is cured after taking one of those pills, people may ask for the same pill, thinking that it will restore their health as well. This goes on until they come upon another medicine that heals one of them, and then everyone wants this new wonder drug. They don't realize that the real cure is the advice of the good doctor who mixed the ingredients in the proper measures. He also prescribed for each patient the right diet, and a regimen for exercise, rest, fresh air, marital relations, and the like.

"The people who lived before the time of Moshe were like the patients duped by the fool. With few exceptions they were misled by astrologers and pseudo-scientists. They wandered from religion to religion, from god to god, until they worshiped a whole pantheon of stars and constellations. In the end, they forgot that the Creator is the One Who guides the stars and the planets for the benefit of mankind. The stars and planets became a source of harm for them, because by worshiping them, they brought on themselves a slew of sicknesses and plagues.

"The world cannot exist without [the Torah; the Torah guides your thoughts toward Godliness and brings you closer to] God. On the other hand, where Torah is missing, harm and destruction will enter."

The Giving of The Torah

80. The Kuzari: "Let's go back to our previous topic[12]. How did your religion start, and how did it grow? How did it manage to gain widespread acceptance in spite of opponents who wanted to suppress it? How long did it take for your faith to become established and securely entrenched? [I cannot believe that an entire nation decided to adopt a new religion on the spur of the moment.] A new religion usually starts with a few individuals who recognize

---

12 The Rabbi digressed when the Kuzari got upset by the statement that the Jews are "God's treasured nation," in paragraph 27.

the spuriousness of their former religion and encourage and support each other in proclaiming the faith that they think God wants them to spread. The number of their followers gradually increases, either because of their own charisma, or because of a ruler who helps their cause by forcing his nation to convert to the new religion, [as was the case with the growth of Christianity and Islam]."

81. The Rabbi: "Only a religion that was invented by a human being develops that way. When the religious movement succeeds, the founder will say he was successful because God supported his mission and taught him, and other such things. But a religion that emanates from the Creator arises all at once. God simply says, 'Let it be,' and it comes into being, as God did when he created the world."

The Exodus

82. The Kuzari: "I am overwhelmed by what you say, Rabbi!"

83. The Rabbi: "It gets even more overwhelming. This started when the Jews were slaves in Egypt, about 600,000 grown men above the age of twenty, all of whom could trace their ancestry to the twelve sons of Yaakov. Not one of them left the faith [to adopt Egyptian paganism], fled to another country, or intermarried with the Egyptians. They all looked forward to the fulfillment of the promise that God made to their ancestors—Avraham, Yitzchok, and Yaakov—that He would give them the land Canaan as an inheritance. At that time, Canaan was populated by seven nations at the peak of their power and prosperity. By contrast, the Jews were at the lowest point of poverty and oppression. Pharaoh killed their babies to stop them from increasing. It was at their darkest hour that God sent Moshe and Aaron, weak as they were, to stand in front of the mighty Pharaoh, where they performed wondrous signs and miracles. Pharaoh was powerless to prevent them from entering his chamber, nor could he do anything to harm them. He could not even save himself from the ten plagues. These plagues began in the water, then polluted the land, the air, the plants, the animals, and finally, affected their bodies and took their lives. In just one instant at midnight, all the firstborn children in each household perished. Except for the Jewish homes, there was not one home without a corpse. All these plagues were preceded by warnings and threats. Moshe announced the exact time when the plagues would strike, and he foretold the moment when they would end each time Pharaoh promised to let the people go. This was done to prove that these plagues were performed by God Who does what He wants, when He wants, and to demonstrate that these were not natural phenomena, nor were they done by the stars, by sorcery, or by chance.

"By God's command the Jews left Egyptian bondage, precisely on the night that the Egyptian firstborn died. They traveled in the direction of the Red Sea, guided by a pillar of cloud by day and a pillar of fire by night.

"Their leader Moshe and their priest Aaron, the two Divinely in-spired men, were eighty and eighty-three years old respectively when they prophesied. Up until that time they had no command-ments other than a few laws they had inherited from Adam and Noach, [namely, the seven Noachide laws that are binding on all mankind]. Moshe did not abolish these laws, rather he added to them [the God-given mitzvos that are binding only on the Jews].

"Pharaoh then pursued the Jews. They did not need weapons [to resist his onslaught]; as a matter of fact, they did not even know how to handle weapons. God split the Red Sea for them, and the Jews crossed on dry land. God then drowned Pharaoh and his army, and cast the Egyptian dead on the shore, in full view of the Jews. This is a long and famous story."

84. The Kuzari: "This certainly had to be an act of God. The Jews did the right thing by accepting the laws that are associated with the Exodus, [like the laws of the Passover offering and the conse-cration of every firstborn], because no one can imagine for a moment that these events were a magic trick or a mirage. Even were you to assume that the Jews did fantasize the plagues and the splitting of the Red Sea, you surely cannot say that their rescue from slavery, the death of their oppressors, and the capture of the spoils which they held on to, were all figments of their imagination. Only the warped mind of a heretic would suggest a thing like that!"

85. The Rabbi: "It is even more astonishing that afterward they wandered through the wilderness for forty years. In this bleak and barren place God fed them [the manna] a newly created food that rained down on them each day except on the Sabbath. This is what they ate for forty years."

86. The Kuzari: "This too, cannot be dismissed as a figment of the imagination. For forty years this bread came down from heaven for 600,000 men and their families, six days a week, except for the Sabbath day. This being so, [that God did not send down the manna on the Sabbath] one must accept the Sabbath as a day of rest, because obviously it is based on a Divine idea."

The Ten Commandments

87. The Rabbi: "We are obligated to keep the laws of the Sabbath because of the manna and because God created the world in six days, and also because [it was included in the Ten Commandments during] an event I am going to discuss with you now.

"Although the Jews believed in Moshe's mission when they witnessed all the miracles, they still had one lingering doubt. How is it possible that God speaks to man? Perhaps these teachings were dreamed up by man, and God approved of the rules this man proposed. He therefore supported him by performing supernatural feats. They could not understand that a spiritual Being could speak. After all—they argued—speech is a physical thing; [you move your larynx, your tongue, your teeth, and your lips when you speak. So how is it possible for God—Who is incorporeal—to speak?]

"God wanted to remove this doubt. So He commanded the Jews [at Mount Sinai] to sanctify themselves spiritually, and physically. God also told them not to come near their wives, preparing themselves to rise to the level of prophecy and readying themselves to hear the words of God directly, without a go-between.

"Three days later wondrous things took place. Thunder and lightning jolted the sky, and fire enveloped Mount Sinai. The fire on the mountain remained and was seen by the people for forty days. They saw Moshe enter the fire and emerge from it. The people heard the Ten Commandments clearly articulated by God. The Ten Commandments are the pillars of the Written Torah and the Oral Torah that is derived from it. One of these commandments was the law of Sabbath, which had been proclaimed earlier in connection with the falling of the manna.

"The people did not receive these Ten Commandments from a singular individual or a prophet. They heard them straight from God Himself. But the people were not able [to endure hearing God's Voice for forty days, as Moshe did when he ascended to Heaven]. From that day on, they firmly believed that Moshe was spoken to by God alone, and that Moshe did not contribute any thought or suggestion of his own to any of the laws.

"Philosophers say that when a person's soul is purified it attaches itself to the Active Intellect—also known as Holy Spirit—or to the angel Gabriel, who then helps it to attain prophetic inspiration. This prophetic inspiration comes to a person in a dream or in a state of semi-consciousness. The person imagines he is hearing words with his soul, not with his ears. He sees visions in his mind, not with his eyes. Philosophers say about such a person that God has spoken to him.

"The momentous event at Sinai gave the lie to these philosophical conjectures. The philosophers' views were completely discredited when God gave Moshe the Ten Commandments inscribed with God's script, engraved on two Tablets hewn of precious stone. The people were able to see God's writing, just as they had heard God's voice. On God's command Moshe then made an Ark for the

Tablets and built the Tabernacle to house it. The Ark remained with the children of Israel as long as there were prophets, close to nine hundred years. This period ended and the Ark was hidden when the Jews disobeyed God, and Nebuchadnezzar conquered the land and led the people into exile."

88. The Kuzari: "If someone hears you say that God spoke with a large throng of your people, and that He wrote Tablets for them and other such anthropomorphisms [attributing human forms to God], he would assume that you believe that God is a tangible being. On the other hand, you cannot be blamed for saying things [like: God speaks, writes, comes down and goes up], because you actually witnessed these awesome events in the company of a large group of people. You are quite right in rejecting the philosophers' analytical, speculative approach to religion, [since your faith is based on things you saw with your own eyes]."

89. The Rabbi: "God forbid! God would never write in the Torah anything causing one to think of God having physical attributes which is completely irrational and untrue. The first of the Ten Commandments bids us to believe in God; the next commandment forbids worshiping other gods, making carved statues, images, or figures [portraying God]. The underlying idea of these two commandments is that we should not attribute any physicality to God.

"How can you suspect that we do not appreciate the exaltedness of God and not understand that He is far removed from physicality. We even elevate some of God's creations above the physical. Take the human soul which is really the essence of every human being. Now, consider the most exalted man that ever lived: Moshe. When Moshe spoke to us, taught us, and led us, the ideas we heard were not produced by his tongue, his heart, or his brain. Those organs were just tools that Moshe's soul used to speak to us. When Moshe spoke, the words he pronounced emanated from his mind and soul. The soul is not physical, nor bound by space. It can conceive of anything that exists in the universe. [Man's imagination has no bounds. His soul has the power to encompass anything it wants, from the end of the universe down to the most minute sub-atomic particle.] We even attribute heavenly characteristics to the soul. If we believe that the human soul is above the physical, surely we believe that God, the Creator of the soul, is above the physical.

"Still, we cannot deny the physical aspects of what happened at Sinai [when God spoke to the Jewish people]. We must say, therefore, that just as we do not understand how the human soul—which is spiritual—expresses itself through speech—which is physical—so too are we unable to fathom how God's will turned into physical speech that penetrated our ears. Neither can we understand how God created [the Tablets] a new physical object from stones that did not exist before, or how He eliminated something from existence [as He did when He created a path through the Red Sea by removing the water]. God does not lack the power [to create or to destroy]. Therefore, we say that He created the Tablets and engraved on them the Ten Commandments, just as He created the heavens—by His utterance alone. God desired it, and the Tablets became solid material the size and shape He wanted, engraved with the Ten Commandments. We also say that He split the Red Sea, and the water rose on the people's right and left like two walls. There were pathways in the middle through which the people could walk without trouble or obstacles. The parting of the water, and its formation into two walls, and the smooth path through the sea, were miracles performed by God. God needed no tool or intermediary to accomplish this, unlike human beings [who need tools and helpers to make their will a reality]. The water stood at God's command alone, and smoothed itself into pathways at His will. The same way, God sends sound waves that form words that express the will of God. These words then reach the ear of the prophet alone or they are heard by the entire people [as was the case at Mount Sinai]."

90. The Kuzari: "Your answer lays to rest [the suggestion that you attribute physicality to God]."

91. The Rabbi: "I'm not saying that this is exactly how these things happened [i.e., the parting of the Red Sea, and the creation of the

Tablets]. Perhaps it came about in a way that is beyond human understanding. Be that as it may, the outcome was that everyone present at the time was convinced that what they were witnessing came directly from God, without an intermediary. The events at Sinai can be compared to Creation; just as the universe was created out of nothing, so were the Tablets and the manna created out of nothing. As a result, those who witnessed these miracles believed in the Torah and became convinced that the world was created by God out of nothing. Thus, these miracles do away with the doubts that are raised by the philosophers who believe that the universe always existed."

THE SIN OF THE GOLDEN CALF

92. The Kuzari: "Be careful, Rabbi. Don't go overboard in praising your people! Don't overlook the famous story of how they rebelled against God in spite of all those miracles. For I have heard that they made a golden calf and worshiped it instead of God."

93. The Rabbi: "The gravity of their sin is in proportion to their greatness. [Their sin was not all that great, but because of their lofty stature it is considered a grave transgression. It takes only a tiny stain to ruin a pure white garment.] Great is he whose sins are counted. [And during the forty years of wandering the Jews sinned only ten times.] "

94. The Kuzari: "You are playing down their faults only because you are partial toward your people. What greater sin is there than idol worship? What virtue could possibly be left after that?"

Historical Overview

95. The Rabbi: "Bear with me for a moment, and let me describe the greatness of the Jewish people. The proof of their greatness lies in the fact that God chose them from all other nations to be His people. They reached a degree of Divine inspiration that made them worthy to hear God's word. This Divine inspiration spilled over onto the Jewish women, so that some of them also became prophets. This is all the more amazing if you consider that, since Adam until that time, only a few isolated individuals attained prophetic inspiration.

"Adam was absolutely perfect in every respect. No one can dispute this, because he was made by the Wise and Almighty Creator, Who chose the raw material and the form Adam would take. There was no flaw in Adam, [like a genetic defect in an ordinary human that might stem] from either father or mother. He had no imperfection that might be due to bad nutrition or poor training in childhood and adolescence; nor were there harmful environmental influences. For God created Adam as an adult, in peak physical and mental condition. Adam's soul and intellect were as good as possible. Furthermore, Adam reached a spiritual level that was above the intellect. He attained a stage that enabled him to connect with God and heavenly beings and comprehend the great truths, just by thinking about them. Because Adam was created by God, we call him, and all his early descendants who resembled him, 'sons of God.'

"Adam had many children, but only one son, Abel, had Adam's spiritual qualities and deserved to take his place. Cain killed his brother Abel because he begrudged him this privilege. God then replaced Abel with Seth who had the Divine spiritual qualities of Adam. That's why Seth was Adam's cherished son; compared to him all the others were like the peel of a fruit. Seth's son Enosh inherited his father's Divine qualities.

"This continued down to Noach. In each generation there were isolated individuals who had Adam's Divine qualities, and who were worthy to be called 'sons of God.' Each was unsurpassed in his physical condition, stature, longevity, wisdom, and capability. By figuring the years of these men we can calculate the time span from Adam to Noach, and from Noach to Avraham.

"There were some individuals in this line who did not measure up to the high standard of Divine quality; Avraham's father,

Terach, for example. But the interrupted line resumed again with Avraham who was a disciple of his grandfather Ever, who had even known Noach. And so the Divine spiritual quality passed from grandfather to grandson.

"Avraham was Ever's cherished descendant and disciple. That's why Avraham is called *HaIvri* [the 'Everite,' i.e., the Hebrew]. Ever, in turn, was the cherished son of Shem, who was the favorite son of Noach. Shem inherited the region of the world with a moderate climate. Situated at the center of this zone in the choice location, was the land of Canaan, the 'land of prophecy.' Of Noach's other two sons, Yefes turned toward the northern, colder zone, and Cham went south, to the tropical region.

"Avraham's cherished son was Yitzchok. Avraham sent his other offspring [Yishmael and the sons of Keturah] away from the land of Canaan, so that it would be set aside solely for Yitzchok. Yitzchok's cherished son was Yaakov. Yaakov's brother Eisav was sent away [by God], because Yaakov was given this land by God [when He said to Yaakov, '*I will give to you and your descendants the land upon which you are laying*" (*Breishis 28:13*)]. All of Yaakov's sons were cherished offspring, for all were worthy to receive Divine inspiration. And so they inherited Canaan, the land that is especially suited for Divine influence.

"For the first time Divine inspiration rested on an entire community, whereas previously it had rested only on individuals. God protected Yaakov's children in Egypt, making them prolific, and greatly increasing their number. They grew like a tree with healthy roots that eventually produces fruit of the same superb quality as the original tree. The original tree was Avraham, Yitzchok, and Yaakov. The fruit of the tree was Moshe, Aaron, and Miriam. It included also, Betzalel and Oholiav [the builders of the Tabernacle], the chiefs of the tribes, and the seventy elders who were worthy of a continuous prophetic spirit, and Joshua bin Nun, Calev ben Yefuneh, Miriam's son Chur, and many more. These people were worthy of having the Divine light shine on them and God's Providence manifesting itself to them.

"If there were sinners [like Terach] among [the generations

from Adam to Avraham], they were spurned by God. Nevertheless, they still were included among the treasured ones, because their fathers and sons were treasured ones. A godless father sometimes is spared because he is a carrier of dormant spiritual characteristics which will surface in his son or grandson. This is what happened in the case of Terach and others. They themselves did not have any spiritual characteristics, but because of their Divinely inspired ancestors they fathered Divinely inspired children. However, such latent spirituality did not exist in the lineage of Cham and Yefes.

"This phenomenon is recognized in the science of genetics where it is found that hereditary traits often skip a generation. Occasionally we see that a son who does not look like his father at all, closely resembles his grandfather. No doubt, recessive genes that lay inert in the father came to full bloom in his son. So too, Ever's genetic material lay dormant in his children until it reappeared in Avraham."

96. The Kuzari: "True, the Jews inherited their greatness from Adam, the most noble creature on earth, which made the Jewish people superior to anyone else in the world. But how can you claim superiority after the sin of the golden calf?"

Explanation of the Golden Calf

97. The Rabbi: "In those days, all the nations worshiped idols. Even if philosophers were to offer proof of monotheism, they would not have given up their idolatry. The masses were taught that a divine influence hovered over idols, giving them supernatural power. Some ascribed this power directly to God. In fact, we ourselves do something like this when we treat certain places with reverence, [like a synagogue or a study hall,] and when we cherish and kiss the dust and stones [of Eretz Yisrael]. Others ascribed the idols' supernatural powers to a star, planet, constellation, or sign of the zodiac. Common folk never accept a doctrine unless it is represented by a tangible symbol that could fire their imagination. [At Mount Sinai] the children of Israel looked forward to receiving something Moshe had promised to bring down from God. They expected something physical that they could see, just as they had gazed at the pillars of cloud and fire when they left Egypt. They had viewed these pillars intently and exalted them by bowing to the Divine Presence dwelling in these pillars. They also bowed to the pillar of cloud that descended on Moshe's tent when God spoke to him.

"The people heard the Ten Commandments, and Moshe ascended the mountain to bring down the engraved Tablets and place them in an Ark. The purpose of the Ark was to give the people a tangible symbol. By gazing at the Ark they would visualize the covenant with God that was written in the Torah scroll, and the Tablets that were created by God out of nothing, that reposed in the Ark. Furthermore, there was a cloud of Divine glory that covered the Ark, and miracles were brought about by the Ark.

"The people waited for Moshe to come down from the mountain, filled with fervent anticipation. All this time they did not change their facial expression, and they remained clothed in the festive attire and adornments they wore on the first day. They patiently waited for Moshe who stayed on the mountain for forty days. He had not brought food with him, and before he left he told them that he would return the same day.[13] [Some came to the conclusion that he died.]

"A small fraction of the people began to argue among themselves about how to deal with Moshe's seeming tardiness. Finally, one faction suggested that they do like other nations and make a tangible object of worship. They did not mean to deny the existence of the God Who had taken them out of Egypt. They merely wanted a symbolic figure in front of them when they related God's miracles, just as the Philistines did when they said that God dwelled in the Ark [they had captured].[14] We ourselves do the same thing when we say that God dwells in heaven, and when we say that

---

13   Rashi offers a different interpretation.
14   1 Samuel, chapters 4,5.

something was an act of God, not caused by accident, human actions, or nature.

"Their sin consisted of making an image which is forbidden by G-d in the Ten Commandments. To make matters worse, they attributed Divine power to something they made themselves without God's approval. Their defense was that they thought Moshe had died, which caused consternation leading them to sin. In fact, the number of those that worshiped the golden calf was no more than 3,000 out of 600,000 adult males.

"The defense Aaron offered [for helping to make the golden calf] was that he wanted to pinpoint the sinners, in order to slay those who would worship the golden calf. Still, he was criticized, because he made the planned rebellion a reality when he threw their gold into the fire, and produced the golden calf.

"By worshiping the calf the Jewish people did not turn completely away from the God Who took them out of Egypt; they merely transgressed a few of God's commandments. God had commanded them not to make images to represent Him, and they made an image anyway. They should have waited longer [for Moshe to come down from the mountain], instead of thinking of another way to bring God's glory into their midst, so that they could worship Him, build an altar and offer sacrifices to Him. This idea came from the fortune tellers and astrologers among them who believed their own ideas made more sense than the true God-given directives. These charlatans acted just like the fool we mentioned above[15] who entered the doctor's office and killed people with medications that could have healed them.

"Although the people followed the astrologers' advice, they did not mean to give up serving God. On the contrary, they believed they had a better way to serve Him. That's why they approached Aaron with their plan, and that's why he was willing to help them. However, this was held against Aaron, because he helped them to implement their plan.

---

[15] Paragraph 79.

"The reason we find the sin of the golden calf so utterly repulsive is because nowadays most nations do not worship idols. But in those days, because all nations made idols for worship it did not seem so unacceptable. Had their sin been that they built a temple of their own design and brought sacrifices and worshiped God according to their own liturgy and ritual, we would not consider it a major offense, because today we build houses of worship and treat them with respect and hope to be blessed through of them. We may go so far as to say that the *Shechinah* rests on our synagogues, and that they are surrounded by angels. If we did not need synagogues as a place to pray, the idea of building a house of worship would sound outlandish to us. For in the days of the Jewish kings [when the *Beis Hamikdash* stood in Jerusalem] it was forbidden to erect a private place of worship, called a *bamah*. The righteous kings of that time used to tear down these *bamahs,* so that people would not pray anywhere except in the *Beis Hamikdash* that God had chosen and designed. On the other hand, there was nothing wrong with the forms of the *cherubim*, because God commanded them to be made and how to form them.

"In spite of these extenuating circumstances, the people who worshiped the golden calf were punished and killed on the same day. Out of the 600,000 men that comprised the people of Israel only 3,000 were killed. However, [in spite of the sin of the golden calf] the manna did not stop falling, the protective cloud did not leave them, nor did the pillar of fire cease to guide them. Prophecy continued to spread and increase among them. Nothing that was granted them was taken from them, except for the two Tablets that Moshe broke. Later when he prayed that they be replaced, he received a second set of tablets, and their sin was forgiven."

THE MITZVOS OF THE TORAH

98. The Kuzari: "You have confirmed the thoughts I had in my dreams, namely: that a person can gain knowledge of God only by acting according to God's command. If this were not so, the many people who try to attain closeness to God would achieve it; even seers, astrologers, fire and sun worshipers and believers in two gods."

99. The Rabbi: "You are right. [Not only the design of the *Beis Hamikdash* was ordained by God], but all our actions are prescribed in the Torah, and these commands were given to Moshe in great detail. He handed them down to the large crowd of people assembled in the desert. They did not need any additional explanations of the Written and Oral Torah, [for Moshe made everything perfectly clear to them]. He also elucidated the laws of the sacrifices: how and where to offer an animal, on which side of the Altar it should be offered, how it should be slaughtered, and what should be done with the blood and the various parts. Everything was clearly defined by God to Moshe, for if even the smallest detail were omitted, the sacrifice would be invalid.

"The same meticulous attention to detail is found in all of nature. Each physical object is made up of a combination of incredibly small molecules. The smallest error in the combination of these molecules would cause irreparable damage to the object, plant, or animal they make up.

"The same way, the Torah indicates how the sacrificed animal should be cut, what is to be done with each limb, which parts should be eaten and which parts burned on the Altar, who should eat it, and who should burn it. The priests are warned not to deviate from the prescribed rules.

"The Torah also lists the physical defects that disqualify a priest, demanding even that there be no imperfection in their vestments and special adornments. This applies especially to the garments of the High Priest who entered the Holy of Holies, on Yom Kippur. This chamber contained the *Shechinah*, the Ark, and the Torah scroll inside the Ark. There are also rules regarding holiness, purity and prayer. It would take too long to mention them all, but every one is based on the Written Torah and the expositions of the Sages of the Talmud which they received orally from the Sages of previous generations, going back to God's words to Moshe.

"Similarly, the specifications for the entire Tabernacle were shown to Moshe on the mountain: the Tabernacle itself, the Tent of Meeting, the Showbread Table, the Menorah, the Ark, the Courtyard, its pillars, its covers, and all its other furnishings. They were all shown to Moshe in spiritual images and he understood how they should look.

"Similarly, Solomon's *Beis Hamikdash* was shown to David in spiritual images. So too, the shape and dimensions of the future *Beis Hamikdash* were shown to the prophet Ezekiel.

"To summarize: As far as serving God is concerned, you cannot innovate, draw inferences, or figure out the reasons for the commandments. If that could be done, the philosophers with their great wisdom and knowledge would have accomplished much more than the Jewish people ever have."

Why Was the Torah Not Given to All Mankind?

100. The Kuzari: "Listening to your proofs, I can easily accept your Torah, without any qualms or misgivings. You demonstrated that a prophet came to an oppressed and enslaved people, promising them freedom from bondage without delay, on a specific date, and in a specific way. He also promised that they would enter the land of Canaan which at that time was occupied by seven mighty nations. He even foretold each tribe's assigned portion in the land before they reached it. Everything came true within a short period of time, accompanied by awesome wonders. This proves the greatness of He Who sent the prophet and the eminence of the prophet who was sent on this mission. It also attests to the magnificence of the nation to whom he was sent.

"[God had good reason to give the Torah to the Jewish people alone and not to all mankind] because, if the prophet claimed that he was sent to right the wrongs of the entire world, he would never be believed. Even if he converted half the world, his mission would be flawed, because he did not accomplish all that God wanted him

to do. [But by giving the Torah only to the Jews, God's will was fulfilled completely]. Another reason [that the Torah was not given to
the rest of mankind is] that the prophet's mission would be ham-
pered by the fact that the Torah is written in Hebrew. [If God intended to give the Torah to the other nations], the prophet would
have to make it intelligible to the nations as far away as Sheba, India
and Khazar, and get them to fulfill what is written in it. It would
take many centuries for these nations to convert to Judaism, unless
they were conquered by the Jews, or they admired the morality of
the Jews who lived among them, or they heard about the miracles
that Moshe performed and became convinced, or a new prophet
would inspire them to adopt the Torah way of life."

101. The Rabbi: "[You are wrong in assuming that God wanted to
give the Torah to all mankind but was prevented for technical reasons. He wanted to give it only to Israel from the very start.]
Moshe appealed only to his people—the nation that spoke his language—to accept the Torah. God promised them that there would
always be prophets to exhort them to keep the Torah. Indeed,
there were prophets during the entire period of the first *Beis
Hamikdash*, when the *Shechinah* dwelled among them.

102. The Kuzari: "But wouldn't God want to improve all mankind? That would be the correct and wise thing to do."

103. The Rabbi: "[By that line of reasoning, you might as well
ask:] Wouldn't it be better if all animals could talk? Obviously you
forgot what I said earlier[16] about how mankind developed from
Adam. I explained that the Divine inspiration came to rest on Seth,
the treasured son of Adam. Only he received the Divine light; the
others were like the peel of the fruit and did not receive it. This
process continued until the sons of Yaakov appeared on the scene.
All the children of Israel were choice individuals, distinguished
from the rest of the world by their holiness. You could say they

---

16 Paragraph 47.

were a separate breed, akin to angels. They all tried to reach the level of prophecy by leading upright, saintly and pure lives and by associating with prophets. Many actually did attain prophecy.

"When someone speaks with a prophet he senses a spiritual renewal. He becomes different from all other people in his yearning for spirituality, his humility and his purity.

"The sense of otherworldly exhilaration such people feel when speaking with a prophet is undeniable proof of the rewards of the World to Come. Such a prophetically inspired person desires only that his soul return to his Divine source, that it divest itself from its physical senses, and joins the highest world. It can then enjoy the vision of the Divine light, and hear the Divine speech. Such an inspired person has no fear of death, because all his physical desires have faded away.

"Since the Torah is a book of teachings that contains wisdom and practices that enable you [in this world] to attain such an exalted level, by following the Torah you can be assured that your soul will live on after the body has passed away."

REWARD IN THE AFTERLIFE

104. The Kuzari: "The afterlife other nations promise is a lot more enticing than yours.[17]"

105. The Rabbi: "They claim their promises will come true after death, while in life there is nothing to indicate that these 'rewards' exist. [But a Jew, as I explained, receives a foretaste in this world of the spiritual delights of the World to Come]."

106. The Kuzari: "I have never seen a believer wish for these rewards to come quickly. To the contrary; were he to delay these rewards a thousand years and remain among the living, he would do so, no matter how miserable his life is."

---

[17] He has in mind the Moslem view of the hereafter as a place of never-ending physical delights.

107. The Rabbi: "But what would you say of a prophet who has visions of overwhelming otherworldly spectacles?"

108. The Kuzari: "Such a person, no doubt, would wish for his soul to remain forever separated from his physical senses, thus continuing to enjoy the rapture of this heavenly light. In fact, he would look forward to dying."

109. The Rabbi: "[The Torah has no need to promise us reward in the afterlife.] The Torah assures us that we will be connected to the Divine influence by means of prophecy or something akin to that. As a result, we will experience magnificent wonders. This is why it does not say in the Torah, 'If you keep this law, I will bring you to gardens of fleshly delights after death.' Rather, it says, "*[If you keep the Torah] I will be a God to you, and you will be a nation [dedicated] to Me, and "I will be your guide*" (*Vayikra* 26:12). Some of you will stand before Me [to serve as priests or Levites], others will ascend to the heavens [i.e, prophets like Ezekiel] and walk among the angels. The angels called Ezekiel "*Son of Man*," so that they could distinguish him from the angels milling around. There will be angels wandering among you on earth. You will see them, sometimes one at a time, sometimes groups of them. They will protect you and do battle for you.

"It says also that you will continue to live in the land that helps you reach this level of spirituality, namely, the Holy Land. Its economy, its years of plenty or famine, will be based on your conduct. [You will be under God's close supervision], while the rest of the world will be guided by the laws of nature. [God pledges that if you observe the Torah,] you will sense the *Shechinah* dwelling among you through the abundance of your crops, through proper rainfall, and through the victories you win over your enemies despite your small number.

"You will recognize that you are not governed by the normal laws of nature, but by God's will [and special supervision]. Conversely, you will discover that if you disobey God's will, you will suffer from drought, epidemics, and wild beasts while the rest of the world enjoys peace and prosperity. In short, you will realize that your lives are governed by a Higher Power, One that transcends nature.

"You will be absolutely sure of these rewards mentioned in the Torah. All these rewards have one thing in common: They bring us closer to God and His angels. One who reaches this level will not be afraid of death. The Torah gives us ample proof of the bliss that comes after death [through the spiritual delights that exist in this world].

"Let me illustrate this with a parable: A large tribe settled somewhere in the desert. One of them left and made his way to India. The king of India received the traveler with pomp and ceremony knowing that, as a member of that clan, he was a descendant of the king's close friend. The king gave him precious gifts to bring to his kinfolk in the desert. He dressed him in exquisite attire, and sent a delegation of officials to escort him. Before sending the guest on his way, the king gave him a set of instructions and made him pledge allegiance to him. The man then traveled back to his tribe in the desert, accompanied by the Indian dignitaries.

"Back in the desert, the tribesmen never imagined that a king would send a group of such distinguished envoys to visit them. They were overjoyed to see their relative again, and they built a magnificent palace to house the king's dignitaries. [Hearing about the gracious king of India,] the tribe sent emissaries to the king's court. Though they had thought that reaching the palace would prove too difficult, they had no trouble because the king's envoys showed them the shortest and easiest route. They realized it was not difficult to go to the king and be admitted to his gracious presence, as long they pledged allegiance to him and paid homage to his envoys. They had no reason to question why they should honor the envoys, because these were the ones who had shown the way to the king's castle.

"The point of the parable is this: The tribe in the desert is the Jewish people. The first one to go to India is Moshe. The later travelers are the prophets. The emissaries of the king are the *Shechinah* and the angels. The exquisite clothing is the spiritual light that rested on Moshe because of his prophecy and the physical radiance that lit up his face. The precious gifts the king sent along are the two Tablets with the Ten Commandments.

"But the believers in other religions [Christianity and Islam which are spin-offs of Judaism] never experienced any of this. The founders of their faiths told them: Pledge allegiance to the king of India, just as the tribe in the desert did, and after you die you will go to the king's palace. Otherwise the king will stay aloof from you now, and torment you after you die. Many of them rejected their faith because they said: No one has ever come back from the dead to tell us that he has gone to heaven or hell. However, the religious leaders used their belief [in heaven and hell] to force the masses to accept their doctrine. They were well aware that their faith was on shaky ground, but they flaunted an image of strong faith, showing off their piety to the ordinary folk. How can [Christian and Moslem spokesmen] boast to the Jews of sumptuous rewards in the here-after, when we experience this reward in this world? After all, our prophets and holy men came closer to life in the World to Come than adherents of other religions, who never reached such a level."

THE JEWS IN EXILE

110. The Kuzari: "I find it hard to believe what philosophers say, that after a person dies, both his body and his soul are destroyed, with only philosophers escaping that fate.

"It is even harder to believe the [Christian and Moslem] doctrine that a person will physically live on forever in paradise just by uttering one phrase, [affirming belief in their deity]. He may know no other phrase all his life, and he may not even understand what he is saying! How great that phrase must be, if it lifts a person from the level of the animals to the level of angels! Conversely, they maintain, that a person who never uttered this phrase goes back to the level of the animals, even if he is a thinker who did nothing but good deeds all his life!"

111. The Rabbi: "We do not deny any person the just reward for his good deeds, no matter what his nationality may be. But the ultimate good is set aside for the nation whose way of life is closest to God. The closer a person is to God during his lifetime, the loftier will be his place in the hereafter."

112. The Kuzari: "Why don't you apply the same line of reasoning to the Jewish people judging their station in the next world by their [alienation from God and their oppressed] status in the world today? [Seen from that vantage point, their status in the hereafter would be very low.]"

113. The Rabbi: "You put us down because of our poverty and degradation, but meekness is precisely the quality that the founders of other religions take pride in. They, [the Christians] exalt the one who said, 'If someone slaps you on the right cheek, turn the other cheek [and let him slap it],' and 'If someone takes your coat, give him your shirt too.' Their founder and his companions were despised, and his followers suffered appalling torture and slaughter for hundreds of years; yet he and the martyrs are revered by [the Christians]. The same is true of the Moslems; [the founder of their religion came from a humble background]. Of course, in the end [Christianity and Islam] became powerful religions. But as powerful as these religions are today, they still glory in the founders of their faith—not in mighty kings with vast empires and powerful armies. In light of that, in our downtrodden state we are closer to God than had we attained greatness in this world."

114. The Kuzari: "That would be so, had you chosen your degradation. But in your case, your humiliation has been imposed on you. If you could, you would destroy your enemies."

115. The Rabbi: "You have touched a sore spot, Khazar king. You are right. Had we learned from our misery to be submissive to God and His Torah, He would not have left us in exile for so long a time. Sadly, only a minority of us realize this. But even so, the majority [who have not learned this lesson] will also receive a reward for bearing the hardship of the exile, no matter whether they do it voluntarily or grudgingly. Any Jew could immediately become a friend of his oppressor by uttering a simple phrase, [affirming his belief in the Christian or Moslem faith]. Such selfless loyalty to God is not over-looked by the Righteous Judge. However, were we to endure this exile and degradation for the sake of God—as we should—we would be the pride of the generation that greets the Messiah, and we would indeed hasten the ultimate redemption for which we long.

"[You mentioned earlier that the other religions promise a glo-rious afterlife to anyone who parrots a simple phrase]. We Jews do not make converts merely by having them recite a formula [of af-firmation]. We require a potential convert to accept acts that are very difficult, such as immersing in a *mikveh*, study, circumcision, the performance of many laws, and adopting our way of life. Bear in mind that circumcision, the Divine symbol ordained by God is placed on the organ of desire, reminding one to control his pas-sion, using it only for proper purposes [to have children], to have marital relations only with a woman permitted to him, at the right time [after she has immersed in a *mikveh*], and at proper intervals. If a person abides by these conditions, he may succeed in produc-ing offspring that will receive Divine inspiration.

"If a convert agrees to with these rules, he and his children will de-light in closeness to God. Nevertheless, a convert is not on par with a Jew from birth, because only Jews from birth can attain prophecy. Converts can become sages and saintly men [like Shemayah and Avtalyon, heads of the Sanhedrin and teachers of Hillel,] who were descendants of converts but they cannot become prophets.

References to Gan Eden and Gehinnom in Tanach

"[Referring to your question[18]] about the delightful pleasures of the hereafter [that are promised by other religions, and which our Torah does not mention explicitly, let me tell you] that long ago,

---

18   Paragraph 104.

our Sages gave detailed descriptions of Gan Eden and Gehinnom, down to reporting such fine points as their length and breadth. They portrayed the joys of Gan Eden and the agonies of Gehinnom in greater detail than the more recent religions do. [I did not mention this before, because] until now I have only spoken about things written plainly in the books of the prophets. They do not discuss the hereafter as broadly as the Sages do. Still, in the books of the prophets it says *'that the body turns to dust after death, and the spirit returns to God Who gave it to man'* (*Koheles* 12:7). Scripture also discusses the revival of the dead which will take place at some point in the future. The resurrection will be announced by the prophet Elijah, who was sent on a mission by God in the past before God took him away. Elijah was bodily raised to heaven, just as God raised others who never tasted death to heaven [like Chanoch who entered Gan Eden without dying]. Furthermore, the Torah cites the prayer of [Balaam] a prophet who prophesied with Divine inspiration, and who prayed to be granted reward in the hereafter *'If only I would die the death of the upright, and my end would be like theirs'* (*Bamidbar* 23:10).

"Also, [Shaul] one of our kings sought advice from the prophet [Shmuel] after he died. Shmuel's spirit foretold all that would happen to Shaul in the future, just as he had prophesied for him when he was still alive. Although communicating with the dead is forbidden in our Torah, this episode shows that the people believed that the soul lives on after the body, and therefore they consulted the dead.

"Consider this: [The beracha of Elokai Neshama,] which opens our morning prayer—is familiar to women and children, not to mention, rabbis—reads:

My God, the soul You placed within me is pure. You created it, You fashioned it, You breathed it into me, You safeguard it within me. Eventually You will take it from me, and restore it to me in time to come. As long as the soul is within me, I gratefully thank You, Lord my God and the God of my forefathers, Master of all works, Lord of all souls. Blessed are You, God, Who restores souls to dead bodies.

"Consider this also: The name 'Garden of Eden' is part of everyone's vocabulary. It was taken from our Torah, and it refers to a spiritual level set aside for Adam. Had he not sinned in Gan Eden [by eating the forbidden fruit], he would have remained there forever. Similarly, Gehinnom is named after a well-known location outside Jerusalem. It is a valley where fire constantly burned, and people burned unclean bones, dead animals, and other unclean things. The word Gehinnom is a combination of the Hebrew words *gei* and *Hinnom* [Valley of Hinnom]."

116. The Kuzari: "If so, then there is nothing new in the descriptions of Gan Eden and Gehinnom the other religions offer. Everything they say is included in your Scriptures. All they did was reiterate and elaborate the things your prophets said long ago."

117. The Rabbi: "Even their expanded version contains nothing new. The Sages have said a great deal on the subject. In fact, you won't find anything in the expositions of the other religions that you cannot find in the words of the Sages."

This concludes Part One, in God's Name.

THE KUZARI

Part II

———✦✦✦———

OVERVIEW OF KHAZAR HISTORY

1. The rest of the Khazar king's story is recorded in the history books of the Khazar people. The king revealed his recurring dream to his army commander, and told him that in his dream he was instructed to go to the Harsan Mountains which are located in the desert near the [Caspian] Sea, there he would find out what actions God favors. The king and his army commander went to these mountains. In the middle of the night, they reached a cave where Jews went every week to observe the Sabbath.[19] The king and his companion identified themselves to the Jews, and eventually they converted to Judaism, and were circumcised in the cave. They returned to their country, determined to live as observant Jews. [Afraid of antagonizing their countrymen,] they kept their conversion a secret. They were careful to reveal their secret only to a few close friends [who also converted and convinced others to embrace the Jewish faith]. The number of converts grew to the point where they were strong enough to make the rest of the Khazars convert to Judaism. They brought in Jewish teachers and religious books and began studying the Torah.

---

[19] Possibly because keeping the Sabbath was forbidden by the government, or they were a group of saintly men who withdrew to the cave to study Torah in isolation.

Khazar history records that the Khazars defeated their enemies and expanded their empire. In their conquests they found vast hoards of hidden treasures, and hundreds of thousands of Khazars adopted the Torah way of life. They loved the Torah, and longed for the *Beis Hamikdash*—so much so, that they constructed a replica of the Tabernacle that Moshe built. They cherished and admired their Jewish-born fellow citizens.

Since the king wanted to study Torah and the Prophets, he took [R. Yitzchak Hasangari], the Rabbi as a teacher and asked him questions about Jewish ideology. He began by asking him about the names and attributes used to describe the Creator, wondering why Jews ascribe human qualities to God, which goes against the Torah and common sense.

DIVINE NAMES AND ATTRIBUTES

2. The Rabbi: "All the names of God, except for the Four-Letter ineffable Name, are characteristics and descriptions of God. We use these attributes to help us form a mental image of God, based on the way we are affected by God's decrees and deeds. We say that God is the Compassionate One, when He improves the condition of a person whose pathetic plight arouses pity in people. Although we call G-d, merciful, you cannot really say this about Him. Rather, He is a righteous Judge Who decrees poverty for one person and wealth for another. His essence is not affected by the decree he renders. He is not merciful toward one, nor angry with another.

"We see the same in human judges. A human judge decides a case according to Torah law. Ultimately, one party wins the case, and the other loses, depending on the judge's verdict. The judge himself, however, [does not adjudicate on the basis of his feelings] and is not affected [by his ruling].

"And so it is with God. Sometimes He will be called 'compassionate and kind' while at other times He will be called, 'jealous and vengeful.' But God is immutable; He never changes from one attribute to another.

"To sum it up: All of God's Names—except for the Four-letter Name—fall into three categories: (a) *active names that describe his actions*, (b) *relative*, and (c) *negative*.

(a) Names that fall in the *active* class describe acts of God that are carried out by natural means, such as '*He makes poor and makes rich; He casts down, He also lifts up,*' *(Shmuel 2:7)* or, God is 'compassionate and kind, jealous and vengeful, mighty, generous,' and other attributes like these.

(b) Names that describe *relative* attributes include: 'Blessed, praised, glorified, holy, exalted, and extolled.' People use these terms when they want to express their reverence of God. Although there are many such names, this does not imply that God is a composite of more than One.

(c) Examples of names in the *negative* category are: 'the living God, the One and Only, the First and Last.' When we praise God as 'the living God' we do not mean that He is 'living' in the sense we humans define 'living.' We use these attributes only in a negative sense, in order to praise God with the negative of their opposites. [Thus when we say that God is 'living' what we mean to say that He is not 'dead.'] To us something is alive when it moves consciously. [When we see an animal move, we know that it is driven by an urge, like hunger or fear. Minerals do not move, so they are not living.] But God is above what we humans define as 'living.'

"We say that God is 'alive' to eliminate the idea of death in reference to Him. When one hears that something is not alive, one immediately thinks it must be dead, though, that is not necessarily so. For example, just because time is not alive does not mean it is dead. Time has nothing to do with either life or death. In the same way, just because a rock is not learned, you cannot call it stupid. Just as a rock is too lowly to be referred to in terms of wise or stupid, so is God too exalted to be thought of in terms of life and death, or light and darkness.

"However, were someone to ask us whether God is light or darkness, we would answer that He is light, afraid that if we said

God was not light, he might think that He must be darkness. We really should answer that the terms light and darkness apply only to physical objects; since God is not physical, the term 'light' applies to Him only in a metaphorical sense, in order to negate the thought that 'darkness' applies to Him.

"Similarly, the concepts of life and death refer only to physical things, and God is above the physical world. When we speak of 'the living God' we simply cannot grasp what this phrase means. And when the Torah says, '*living God*' it does so to place God in contrast to idols, which are dead gods, that cannot do anything.

"In the same way, we say that God is 'One,' in contrast to the idea of two or more gods, not to ascribe to Him oneness the way we understand it. When we say 'one' we mean that all the parts of an object have been assembled into a unit, such as 'one bone,''one arm,' 'one sinew,' 'one breath of air,' or 'one body of water.' Time too, can be broken down into parts, such as 'one day' or 'one year.' By contrast, the Divine essence is above any kind of merging or dividing. The Torah says that God is One, as opposed to the idea of many gods.

"Likewise, God is called 'First' in order to exclude the idea that there was something before God, but not to say that He has a beginning, [for God has always existed]. So too, God is called 'Last' to reject the notion that He has an end, not to set a time limit for Him, [for God is eternal and everlasting].

"All these attributes have no bearing on God's true essence; do not read into them the idea that God is multi-faceted.

Overt and Covert Miracles

"On the other hand, all attributes that relate to the Four-Letter Name describe His power to create without using the forces of nature as intermediaries. For example, in the passages, '*I am the One Who forms light and creates darkness*' (*Yeshayah 45:7*)', and, '*To*

Him Who alone performs great wonders' (Tehillim 136:4), the word 'alone' means that He brings these things into being by His decree and His will alone, without the use of an intermediary.

"Perhaps this is what God meant when He said to Moshe, '*I revealed Myself to Avraham, Yitzchok and Yaakov as* El Shaddai' *(Shemos 6:3)*. [This Name implies power and triumph.] God protected the Patriarchs who were strangers surrounded by hostile pagans. He granted them victory over their adversaries, [but He did it in a hidden way, through miracles that looked like "natural" developments.] As it says, '*He let no man rob them, and He rebuked kings for their sake' (Divrei Hayamim 16:21)*. God did not create overt miracles for the Patriarchs as He did for Moshe, that is why the verse continues, '*But I did not make Myself known to them by My Name Hashem.*' The Name *Hashem* implies God's miraculous intervention, while *Shaddai* denotes God's guidance through natural means. God protected the Patriarchs only in natural ways.

"The wonders God performed for Moshe and Israel left no doubt that it was the Creator of the world Who generated these [supernatural] wonders, such as the plagues of Egypt, the splitting of the Red Sea, the manna, the pillar of cloud, and other miracles. The reason for these overt miracles was not that the children of Israel were greater than Avraham, Yitzchok, and Yaakov. Rather, they were a large throng of people, who harbored doubt about God. The Patriarchs, on the other hand, were men of unwavering faith and pure character. Even had they experienced nothing but misfortune all their lives, their faith in God would not have been shaken. Therefore they did not need such visible miracles.

"God is also described as, 'Wise of Heart' because He is the source of all wisdom. Wisdom is not one of His attributes [because He Himself is the essence of wisdom]. The continuation of the verse, '[He is] immensely strong,' falls in the 'active' category of attributes, [signifying the strength of God seen through nature.]"

Physical Attributes

3. The Kuzari: "How do you explain those Divine attributes that are even more physical than the above, such as [God] sees, hears, speaks, writes the Tablets, comes downs on Mount Sinai, rejoices in His works and has heartfelt sadness?"

4. The Rabbi: "[As far as God rejoicing and grieving is concerned,] I compared God [in paragraph 2] to an impartial judge who is not swayed by emotions. Still, when He issues a decree bringing prosperity and prestige, people will say that He loves them and is happy for them. And if he rules that their houses be demolished and their cities laid to waste, people will say, that He hates them and is angry with them. [Yet the judge is not motivated by love or hate; he simply passes sentence according to the law. It is the same with God.]

"[To answer your question about God hearing, seeing and writing, let me explain:] The air and the other elements function according to God's will. They can therefore be formed into Divine speech or writing. [Speech reaches the human ear by way of sound waves; thus God can bend the air into sound waves that form spoken words.] The same way, heaven and earth were formed by God's will. This explains why we say that God 'writes' or 'speaks.'

"[To explain how we can say, 'God came down', understand that] there is an etherial, delicate substance that envelops a spiritual core [like the body encloses the soul]. We call this the 'Holy Spirit,' [and this is what a prophet sees in his vision]. When the Torah says, '*The glory of God rested on Mount Sinai*' (*Shemos 24:16*), it means the spirit enclosed inside this rarified substance [that can be perceived by the human eye]. Figuratively and for the sake of brevity, this image is referred to simply as 'God.' This is what the Torah means when it says, "*God came down on Mount Sinai*" (*Shemos 19:20*). We will discuss this in depth when we deal with metaphysics."

God's Will and Desire

5. The Kuzari: "You have laid to rest all doubts that God's attributes suggest physicality, and you have proven that God's Oneness is indivisible. But how do you explain the attribute of Divine will? Philosophers say that God does not desire [because if one desires he is lacking the object of his desire which cannot be said about God.]"

6. The Rabbi: "If this is all that is bothering you, victory is in sight. We would answer the philosopher, 'What makes the heavenly spheres constantly revolve in circles? What makes the outer sphere [the ninth sphere] encircle all others while it itself floats in nothingness? What makes it stay on course without swerving from its orbit? What causes the earth to be at the center of all [nine] spheres without straying off course or going around in an orbit of its own?[20] What keeps order throughout the universe—which you can plainly see when you look at every object in nature? One has to admit [that everything was created with a well-defined plan]. You cannot tell me that these things created themselves, or that they created each other. [They were obviously created that way by the will of God.]

"Whatever willed these things into being also willed the air to form sound waves that made the Ten Commandments audible to the Jewish people, and willed that the words appear, and become engraved on the Tablets. You may call it 'God's Will' or 'God's Utterance,' or whatever you feel [conveys the idea that it was created by God's design]."

7. The Kuzari: "I appreciate the deeper meaning of the Divine attributes, and I understand the concepts of 'the glory of God,' 'angels of God,' and the 'Presence of God.' These are terms prophets

---

[20] The ancients assumed that the earth was the central body around which the sun, planets, and the celestial bodies revolved. They believed that the earth was stationary and the planets were fastened to nine concentric rotating spheres.

use to describe the things they see in their visions. For example, *a pillar of cloud, a consuming fire, a thick cloud, mist, fire,* and *brightness.*'

"Let me give you an analogy [to explain how sparks of Divine radiance are perceived by prophets here on earth]: Early in the morning or during twilight it is light outside although the sun has sunk below the horizon. Or on a cloudy day it is light even though the sun is hidden. People say that the light comes directly from the sun, but this is not so. The minute particles in the clouds and atmosphere above us absorb the sun's light and in turn these particles shine their light on us."

8. The Rabbi: "True. So too, the 'glory of God' is a reflection of Divine light, which showers favor on His people and His land."

9. The Kuzari: "I can understand that you say that His people are shown God's favor. But why do you say that His land is favored?"

ERETZ YISRAEL, THE PRECIOUS LAND

10. The Rabbi: "You should not find it hard to understand how one land can be superior to all other lands. Certain plants thrive better in one place than in another, and certain minerals, gems or animals are found in one country but not in another. The natives of one region differ racially and culturally from those of another region. Furthermore, since perfection or deficiency of the soul depends [to an extent] on the physical well-being and balance of the body, it is no wonder that certain lands tend to produce men of higher spiritual perfection than others."

11. The Kuzari: "I have never heard that the inhabitants of Eretz Yisrael are of a higher caliber than other people."

12. The Rabbi: "What about your mountain that you say produces exquisite vines. Had you not planted the vines, or neglected to cultivate the land, it would not yield any grapes.

"Eretz Yisrael's outstanding qualities are evident first and foremost in the people which are the essence and heart of all nations, as I have mentioned earlier.[21] [They are like the exquisite vines.] Secondly, the land thrives through the service of God and the observance of the laws [of the Torah] that are connected with it, which can be compared to the tilling of the vineyard. This treasured nation could never attain their spiritual excellence anywhere else, just as the vineyard cannot thrive anywhere but on this mountain. [Unfortunately, the Jewish nation and this observance is lacking today, which is why you do not detect excellence in the people of Eretz Yisrael.]"

13. The Kuzari: "How can you say that [only Eretz Yisrael produces a superior breed of people? Many prophetic revelations took place outside Eretz Yisrael.] From Adam to Moshe, there were prophets in other countries: Avraham prophesied in Ur Kasdim, Ezekiel and Daniel both prophesied in Babylonia, and Jeremiah in Egypt!"

14. The Rabbi: "Whoever prophesied did so either in Eretz Yisrael or concerning Eretz Yisrael. Avraham's prophesy outside Eretz Yisrael was concerning the instructions to walk through the Land; Ezekiel foretold that the Jews would eventually return to Eretz Yisrael from the Babylonian exile. Daniel and Yechezkel prophesied about the future of Eretz Yisrael [and the ultimate ingathering of the exiles.] Another reason why Ezekiel and Daniel were able to prophesy outside Eretz Yisrael is that both were present at the First Temple and perceived the *Shechinah* that dwelled there. This perception endowed a person who was duly prepared, to continue with the lofty level of prophecy.

"You may ask: How about Adam? [Who it seems prophesied outside of Eretz Yisrael.] The answer is: According to our tradition,

---

[21] 1:47 and 1:49.

Eretz Yisrael was the land from which Adam was created and the
land where he died. The Gemara tells us that there are four couples
buried in the Cave of Machpelah [which is in Eretz Yisrael]: Adam
and Eve, Avraham and Sarah, Yitzchok and Rivkah, and Yaakov and
Leah.

Age-old Rivalry Over Eretz Yisrael

"Eretz Yisrael is the land called 'in front of God'. The Torah says
about Eretz Yisrael, '*It is a land that is constantly under God's
scrutiny*" *(Devarim 11:12)*. It is the land that gave rise to the jeal-
ousy between Cain and Abel. They wanted to know which of them
would be Adam's successor as the treasured and beloved one. The
one chosen would inherit Eretz Yisrael becoming linked to the
Divine influence, while the other would be of little significance, like
the peel of a fruit. Cain killed his brother Abel out of jealously, and
Adam was left without an heir. We read in the Torah that '*Cain left
God's Presence,*' *(Bereishis 4:16)*, which means that he was driven
out of Eretz Yisrael, and became a restless wanderer.

"Scripture uses the same expression in connection with Jonah.
It says, '*Jonah started out to flee to Tarshich from God's Presence,*'
(Jonah 1:3) which means he fled from the land of prophecy [so that
he would not have to prophesy against Nineveh]. But God brought
him back to Eretz Yisrael in the belly of a fish, and he prophesied
there.

"Adam's son Seth was born with his father's characteristics, as it
says, '*[Adam] had a son in his likeness and form, and he named him
Seth*' *(Bereishis 5:3)*, [which means that he was on Adam's spiritual
level]. Seth replaced Abel as the most esteemed descendant, as it
says, '*[Adam said:] God has provided me with another son in place
of Abel*' (Bereishis 4:25). Seth was therefore worthy to be called
'son of God,' just like Adam. He was given Eretz Yisrael which is
one level below Gan Eden.

"Later it was Yitzchok and Yishmael who vied for the possession of Eretz Yisrael. Yishmael was removed from the Land, like the peel from a fruit. But God did not deny Yishmael any worldly goods. God said, '*I will bless him, and make him fruitful*' *(Bereishis 17:20)*, referring to material wealth. But regarding Yitzchok it says in the next verse, '*But I will keep My covenant with Yitzchok*' *(Bereishis 17:21)*, meaning that Yitzchok would receive the gift of Divine prophecy and the blessings of the World to Come. Neither Eisav nor Yishmael was included in the Divine covenant, nevertheless, they both enjoyed material prosperity to a great degree.

"Next a dispute arose between Yaakov and Eisav over the birthright and the blessings, which included Eretz Yisrael. Eisav was pushed aside in favor of Yaakov, despite Eisav's physical prowess and Yaakov's weakness.

"[You argued that Jeremiah prophesied in Egypt, outside Eretz Yisrael,] but Jeremiah's prophecy was [not outside Eretz Yisrael]. In fact, he prophesied in the portion of Egypt that is part of Eretz Yisrael, and he prophesied for the sake of Eretz Yisrael. The same was the case with Moshe, Aaron and Miriam who prophesied in Paran which is also part of Eretz Yisrael. The Sinai desert and Paran belong to Eretz Yisrael, because they are east of the Red Sea. The Torah defines the borders of Eretz Yisrael, saying, "*I will set your borders from the Red Sea to the Philistine Sea, and from the desert to the river*" *(Shemos 23:31)*. The 'desert' in this verse refers to Paran Desert which the Torah describes as '*the great and awesome desert*' *(Devarim 1:19)*. This is the southern border of Eretz Yisrael. The 'river' in this verse refers to the Euphrates River which is the northern border of Eretz Yisrael.

"[Proof that Eretz Yisrael is the Holy Land can be seen from the fact that] the altars the Patriarch erected were all in Eretz Yisrael. The binding of Yitzchok took place on the desolate mountain, Mount Moriah. It says, '*Avraham named the place "God Will See."* *Today it is therefore said, "On God's Mountain He will be seen"*' *(Bereishis 22:14)*. The Book of Chronicles tells us explicitly that the Beis Hamikdash was built on Mount Moriah *(Divrei Hayamim 3:1)*.

"[More proofs of the sanctity of Eretz Yisrael:] "Not until the

time of David, when Mount Moriah was already inhabited, with
Aravnah the Jebusite tilling its soil there, was it revealed that this
place was selected as the dwelling place for the *Shechinah*. [Before
the land was conquered and settled by the Jews there was no sanctity attached to it.]

"Only in Eretz Yisrael are there sites called 'the Gates of
Heaven'. Yaakov, for example did not attribute his prophetic vision
[of the ladder that reached from earth to heaven] to the purity of
his soul, or his deep faith and integrity, but to the significance of
the place itself. When he awoke he said, '*How awe-inspiring this
place is! This is none other than the House of God, and this is the Gate
of Heaven*' (*Bereishis 28:17*). And earlier it says, '*He came to the
place,*' (*Bereishis 28:11*) meaning, the place especially chosen [as the
site of the Beis Hamikdash].

"When Avraham, the very root of the chosen Jewish people, was
found worthy of Divine revelation, God removed him from his
birthplace and sent him to the one land where he could attain perfection. Let me give you an analogy: If a farmer finds a fruit bearing tree in the desert, he transplants it into a properly irrigated or-
chard to make it thrive. The fruit then has a delicate rather than
coarse flavor and the tree produces a bountiful crop year after year,
rather than a meager yield once every few years. The farmer is successful only if he transplants the tree at the proper time, in the
proper place. In the same way, the gift of prophecy flourished
among Avraham's descendants only when they were living in Eretz
Yisrael, and only when they fulfilled the required conditions for
prophecy, namely: purity, Divine service, sacrificial offerings, and
observance of all the commandments.

"The factor that contributed most to attaining prophecy was the
fact that the *Shechinah* dwelled in the Beis Hamikdash. It was as if
the *Shechinah* was looking for people worthy to attach themselves
to God.

"This is similar to what philosophers call the Active Intellect,
which seeks out someone whose character is perfect and is ready to
receive perfect wisdom. The same way, the human soul seeks an em-
bryo in the mother's womb when it is mature enough to receive the

soul. Similarly, the life force which makes plants grow, seeks out [the seed], a physical object, and it becomes a growing, living plant."

15. The Kuzari: "These are philosophical issues that need to be studied in depth, but now is not the time. Today, please, continue your discussion of the advantages of Eretz Yisrael."

The Greatness of Eretz Yisrael

16. The Rabbi: "Eretz Yisrael was selected to guide the whole world, [since it is the place from which wisdom emanates], but ever since the time of the Dispersion [during the generation that built the Tower of Babel], it was set aside specifically for the Jewish people. As it says, "*When the Most High gave nations their heritage and split up the sons of man*" *(Devarim 32:8).*

"In spite of all his great virtues, even Avraham was not worthy of entering into a covenant with God and of gaining Divine influence until he entered Eretz Yisrael. It was there that God made with him the Pact between the Halves (Bereishis 15:17). If Eretz Yisrael has the power to elevate Avraham—a lone individual—all the more so will this happen to a 'chosen people,' a nation that is called the 'people of God' who live in the land that is called the 'Inheritance of God'. And surely they deserve that God manifests Himself to them [on the Jewish holy days]. They observe these holy days at times established by God, not on dates picked at random or arrived at by astronomical calculations [like secular holidays]. These holy days are therefore called 'festivals of God.' They perform the sacrificial offerings and other precepts commanded by God, according to the laws of purity. These acts are called '*The work of God*' *(Divrei Hayamim I 26:30)* and the '*service of God*'" *(Bamidbar 8:11).*

17. The Kuzari: "Under those circumstances it is certainly appropriate for the glory of God to appear to the nation known as 'the Nation of God.'"

18. The Rabbi: "You can recognize the importance of Eretz Yisrael in that it was given its own Sabbath. For it says, '*A complete Sabbath for the land,*' *(Vayikra 25:4)* and '*The land shall observe a Sabbath for God*' *(Vayikra 25:2)*. Also, the land may not be sold permanently, for it says, '*No land shall be sold in perpetuity, since the land is Mine*' *(Vayikra 25:23)*. Furthermore, the timing of the Sabbath and the holy days depends on Eretz Yisrael, because it is situated in the center of the world."

THE INTERNATIONAL DATELINE

[Introductory note: The following remarks will be helpful to better understand the coming paragraphs.

There is a point on the globe where the new day starts. To illustrate this point: If you travel on an airplane that flies at the speed of the sun, and you begin in New York, Monday at 8 a.m, three hours later, you are in Los Angeles, where it is also 8 a.m. As your flight progresses, the time remains at 8 a.m. If you circle the globe and return to New York it will be 8 a.m., on Tuesday morning. Where did the day change from Monday to Tuesday? The secular world has adopted the international dateline as the dividing line. It runs through the center of the Pacific Ocean from north to south. If it is, Sunday 8 a.m. east of that line, when you cross that line, it is Monday 8 a.m., because the new day starts at the international dateline. The Rabbi explains that the east coast of China is the dateline; there the new day starts.

During Creation, the place where it became Shabbos for the first time was Eretz Yisrael. When the sun set at the end of the sixth day of Creation, the first Shabbos started in Eretz Yisrael. That means that in China[22] the first Shabbos started 18 hours later. By the time Shabbos begins Friday evening at 6 p.m. in China, it is already 12 p.m. Shabbos noon in Eretz Yisrael.]

---

[22] The Chazon Ish maintains that what is meant by China is off the coast of China.

19. The Kuzari: "But we calculate the day to start in China, [not in Eretz Yisrael] because the east coast of China is the beginning of the Asian continent, the place where the populated area of the world begins."

20. The Rabbi: "Nevertheless, the Jews observed the first Shabbos in Sinai; to be more precise, in Alush, which is where the manna fell for the first time. [Therefore, Shabbos begins in Alush which is inside the territory of Eretz Yisrael.] After Shabbos began at sunset in Sinai, it moved west—with the setting sun—and traveled across all the places that are west of Sinai, until Shabbos came to China which is on the eastern rim of the Asian continent. Thus, Shabbos began in China eighteen hours after it began in Eretz Yisrael. Because Eretz Yisrael lies at the center of the populated area of the world, when the sun set there [at 6 p.m.], it is midnight in China. And when it is noon in Eretz Yisrael, the sun is setting in China, and the new day is just beginning.

"This [eighteen-hour time difference] is the principle underlying our system of determining the new month. Our Sages say, 'If the *molad* [i.e., the conjunction of the moon] occurs before midday, the new moon becomes visible near sunset (Rosh Hashanah 20b). The Sages were referring to the time of the *molad* in Eretz Yisrael, where the Torah was given, [because Mount Sinai lies in the territory of Eretz Yisrael.] Adam was transferred from Gan Eden to Eretz Yisrael on the eve of Shabbos; there the counting of time began, on the first Friday evening at the end of the six days of Creation. There Adam first started to reckon and give names to the days of the week. As the population of the world spread, everyone continued counting the days of the week as Adam did. That's why there is no disagreement among the nations of the world about the seven-day week, [and about what day of the week it is].

"Don't quote people, saying, the day starts at noon [90 degrees west of Eretz Yisrael, at which time it is sunset in Eretz Yisrael. They calculate in this manner because they say that the first light was created in the west, and it was there that the sun began to orbit. We also believe that God created the light [90 degrees west] but being so it immediately set in Eretz Yisrael. We begin our day with the beginning of night, as it says, '*It was evening and it was morning, one day*' *(Bereishis 1:4)*. And the Torah decrees, '*From evening to evening shall you rest on your day of rest*' *(Vayikra 23:32)*. [So although we are in agreement as to the position of the sun at its creation, we give import to the point of the first sunset which was over Eretz Yisrael.]

"Astronomers [like Ptolemy] who calculated that the day begins in China] are merely copying the works of others. They found obscure writings on astronomy in ancient Jewish texts which they could not understand. They decided the day begins in China, which disagrees with most of what the Torah says—but not entirely. The Torah Sages do agree that the first day's daylight began when the sun reached China. The difference between our view and theirs is that we count the night before the day, [and the first sunset was in Eretz Yisrael].

"The eighteen hour [time difference between Eretz Yisrael and China] must be made the basis for deciding what day of the week it is. Eretz Yisrael, which is where we began to count the days of the week, is six hours [i.e. 90 degrees] east of the place where the sun was when the days were named. So, Adam gave the name Shabbos at the beginning of the day on which the sun set to the west of him. Adam—who was in Eretz Yisrael—saw the sun setting and called this the beginning of Shabbos. The hour of the 'beginning of Shabbos' continued to move around the globe until Adam saw the sun in the sky above him [Shabbos at noon] which happened eighteen hours later. At that moment it was evening—the beginning of Shabbos—in China, and this was the last place on earth where it was the 'beginning of Shabbos.' Any place west of that point is considered to be east of Eretz Yisrael, the point where the day starts.

"There must be a place on the globe where east begins and west ends. This place is Eretz Yisrael, the time zone where the day begins. This is also essential from the point of view of natural science. It would not be realistic for all populated areas of the world to have the same name for the day of the week unless we fix one place on the globe that marks the beginning of the day, where east begins, and west ends. If we did not have such a demarcation line, we would never be able to have definite names for the days of the week, since any point on the globe would be east and west at the same time; [east to the area west of it, and west to the area east of it]. For example, China would be east in relation to Eretz Yisrael, but west in relation to [America and] Europe. There would be no absolute east or west, no beginning or end, and consequently, there would be no definite names for the days of the week. But when you have an international dateline, you can have definite names for the days, with Eretz Yisrael as the starting point."

Time Zones

"We have to divide the globe into time zones, because it is impractical to set a separate time for each longitudinal point on earth. Jerusalem itself has an infinite number of longitudinal points; without time zones, if you walked in an easterly direction from, Mount Zion to the site of the Beis Hamikdash, [you would have to move your watch ahead every second.] Taking this one step further, you certainly would [have to reset your watch] if you traveled from Damascus to Jerusalem, [which is about half a degree longitude west of Damascus]. We must say that Shabbos in Damascus [which is east of Jerusalem] begins earlier than in Jerusalem, and by the same token, Shabbos in Jerusalem must start earlier than in Egypt. Therefore, we establish time zones, [so that all locations within a time zone keep the same day.]

"The difference between the first and the last time zone on any given day is eighteen hours; no more, no less. If the people in the first time zone call the day Shabbos, then, when the 'beginning of Shabbos' leaves their time zone, it moves into the next zone, and so on. This continues for eighteen hours after Shabbos began in the first time zone, at which time the sun is high in the sky in Eretz Yisrael. [When Shabbos begins at 6 p.m. Friday evening in China, it is 12 p.m. Shabbos noon, in Eretz Yisrael.] China is the last point on earth where Shabbos begins, so from that point on, no one else in the world will say, 'Right now is the beginning of Shabbos.'

The Molad[23]

"Our Sages had this in mind when they said, 'If the *molad* [i.e., the conjunction of the moon] occurs before midday, the new moon becomes visible near sunset.' They meant: If the *molad* occurs before noon on Shabbos in Jerusalem, we can be sure that [somewhere in the world] the new moon will be visible on Shabbos near sunset. For eighteen hours there will be people somewhere in the world, who call the day Shabbos. It remains Shabbos in China until the sun is at high noon [on Sunday] in Eretz Yisrael, eighteen hours after the entire night and day of Shabbos in Eretz Yisrael. Consequently, the moon becomes visible for the first time to someone who is on the east coast of China on Shabbos evening.

"This follows the rule of the Sages: 'It is necessary that a full night and a full day should be part of the new month' (*Rosh Hashanah 20b*). [If this conjunction occurred any later than noon in Eretz Yisrael which is the beginning of Shabbos in China it would] mean that the moon would not be visible anywhere in the world while it is still Shabbos. If the *molad* takes place later than Shabbos noon in Eretz Yisrael, it will no longer be Shabbos for the required twenty-four hour period anywhere in the world.

"The Sages wanted to make sure [with their rule] that the name

---

23 Rosh Chodesh is the day the new moon first becomes visible. The time that the moon actually passes in front of the sun is called the conjunction. In Hebrew this is called the molad. The new moon is not visible until 24 hours after the conjunction because the surface that is visible is too small to reflect the sun's light. Therefore Rosh Chodesh cannot be proclaimed until 24 hours after the molad. But since the time of the molad is calculated by the time in Yerushalyim even if it occurs at 12 noon at this time it is just the beginning of the day in China so that 24 hours later when it can first be seen it is the end of that same day in China. This makes it a day which can become Rosh Chodesh.

of the day of the week would be the same all over the world. Asking a person in China and one who lives in a western country: 'On what day did you fix Rosh Hashanah?', you would receive the same answer. This is despite the fact that for one of them, the holy day had already passed while the other is still celebrating the festival. Both of them observed the festival on the same day of the week."

More Proofs of the Magnificence Of Eretz Yisrael

"All calculations regarding the fixing of the Sabbaths and the festivals depend on Eretz Yisrael which is called *the inheritance of God, His holy mountain, God's Footstool, the Gate of Heaven,* and about which it says, *From Zion will the Torah come forth.*

"[You also can tell how important Eretz Yisrael is by the fact that] the Patriarchs were eager to live in Eretz Yisrael, though it was ruled by the Canaanites. Yaakov and Yosef yearned for Eretz Yisrael and asked that their remains be buried there. Moshe pleaded for the privilege of entering the Land, and when his plea was rejected he considered it a grave punishment and a misfortune. [In fact Moshe kept insisting,] until he made God angry. Subsequently he was granted the privilege of seeing Eretz Yisrael from the summit of Mount Pisgah, which he considered a great favor.

"Persians, Indians, Greeks, and people of other nations used to send their offerings and asked to be prayed for in the holy Temple. [Even great rulers like Cyrus and Darius,] while believing in a different religion—after all, their ancestors did not receive the Torah—contributed generously to the rebuilding of the Beis Hamikdash. To this day, gentiles pay homage to Eretz Yisrael, even though the *Shechinah* is no longer there. People of many nations make pilgrimages to Eretz Yisrael and want the Land for themselves. We are unable to do so, because of our exile and oppression. [These are some of the praises of Eretz Yisrael mentioned in Scripture, but] I couldn't possible tell you all of the Rabbis' tributes; it would take up too much time."

The Rabbis Pay Tribute to Eretz Yisrael

21. The Kuzari: "Please, tell me a few things the Rabbis said about Eretz Yisrael."

22. The Rabbi: "Here are a few examples: 'All may be forced to move to Eretz Yisrael, but they may not be forced to leave Eretz Yisrael.' [Meaning, a husband may compel his household to move with him to Eretz Yisrael, but he cannot force them to leave with him, if he wants to emigrate].' They further decreed: If a husband wants to leave his country for Eretz Yisrael and his wife refuses, he may divorce her without paying her *kesubah* [marriage settlement]. On the other hand, if the wife wants to move to Eretz Yisrael and the husband refuses to join her, he must divorce her and pay her *kesubah*.

"They also said: 'It is better to live in Eretz Yisrael, in a town of non-Jews, than abroad in a town inhabited by Jews; for anyone living in Eretz Yisrael is considered as though he has a God, while anyone living abroad is considered as though he has no God. [To prove the point, when David was chased out of Eretz Yisrael by Saul], he said, *"They have driven me away this day from attaching myself to the heritage of God, as if to say, "Go worship the gods of others"* (Shmuel I 26:19). You see, whoever lives outside Eretz Yisrael is compared to an idol worshiper.

"Egypt was included in the covenant of inheritance God promised the children of Avraham, as it says, *'To your children I have given this land, from the River of Egypt to the great river, the Euphrates'* (Shemos 23:31). Therefore, our Sages said: 'If it is forbidden to return and live in Egypt—a country that was included in the covenant—then it surely is forbidden to live in other countries'.

"Another saying is: 'Whoever is buried in Eretz Yisrael is considered to be buried under the altar' (Kesubos 111a). The Rabbis considered one who lived, died and was buried in Eretz Yisrael more deserving of praise than one who was brought there for burial. They said: 'Receiving a man in his lifetime is not the same as receiving him after death' (Kesubos 112a).

"The Rabbis said concerning a person who had the opportunity to live in Eretz Yisrael but chose not to, that his remains may not be accepted for burial in Eretz Yisrael. They applied to such a person the verse, '*[God says:] "While you lived you made My heritage an abomination, and in death you came and defiled My land"'* (*Yirmiyah 2:7*).

"Another example: [One who lived in Eretz Yisrael, whose brother had died childless outside Eretz Yisrael wanted to fulfill the obligation of *yibbum* (marrying his brother's childless widow). He asked R. Chanina whether he was permitted to leave Eretz Yisrael to perform the *yibbum*]. R. Chanina replied, 'His brother married a heathen, and he died. Blessed be the Almighty Who killed him. And you want to follow him!' [Since he left Eretz Yisrael, he and his wife are considered idol worshippers and therefore heathens. (*Maharsha*)]

"Another example: The Rabbis prohibited selling real estate in Eretz Yisrael to a heathen, or allowing a house or land in Eretz Yisrael to fall into disrepair.

"Another example: The Rabbis ruled that a Jewish court outside Eretz Yisrael may not rule on civil cases involving monetary penalties. Also, the slave of a Jew may not be sold to someone outside of Eretz Yisrael.

"Another example: The Rabbis said: The air of Eretz Yisrael makes you wise. They also said: Whoever walks four cubits in Eretz Yisrael is assured of a place in the World to Come.

"When R. Zeira came to Eretz Yisrael and could not find a solid bridge to cross the Jordan River, he grabbed a rope and crossed on a frail plank bridge. When a passing heretic mocked him, criticizing his foolhardiness, R. Zeira replied, ['I was rushing because] Who could assure me that I would be worthy of entering the Land which even Moshe and Aaron were not worthy of entering?'

Why Don't You Move to Eretz Yisrael?

23. The Kuzari: "If all these things are true, [and Eretz Yisrael is indeed such a glorious place], then your love of the Land leaves much to be desired. Eretz Yisrael is not your primary concern. You haven't tried moving there nor did you prepare to make it your resting place after death. Yet you say [in your blessings after the Haftarah], '*Have mercy on Zion for it is the source of our life*,' and you believe that the *Shechinah* will return there. [And although it has not yet returned,] the fact that the *Shechinah* dwelled in Eretz Yisrael for 900 years,[24] should be reason for any devout Jew to go there. One is spiritually uplifted there, just as one is uplifted in the presence of holy men, for it is the *gate to heaven*.

"All nations agree on this point. Some gentiles even say that Eretz Yisrael is the place where souls are gathered before they are taken to heaven. Moslems believe it's the place where their prophet went to heaven, and where Judgment Day will take place. In fact, all religions make Eretz Yisrael the focal point of their worship.

"Perhaps your knee-bending and bowing toward Eretz Yisrael is a hollow gesture and a meaningless ritual. Your ancestors [Avraham, Yitzchok, and Yaakov] preferred to live in Eretz Yisrael rather than in their birthplaces. They preferred living as strangers there, rather than as citizens in their own country. This, even though the *Shechinah* had not yet appeared there, and the country wallowed in immorality and idol worship. Even during times of famine, they left Eretz Yisrael only by the word of God. And—[as in the case of Yaakov and Yosef]—they gave instructions to have their remains brought there [from Egypt] for burial."

24. The Rabbi: "You have touched a raw nerve, King of Khazar. The sin [of failing to go back to Eretz Yisrael] is what prevented the fulfillment of God's promise that the *Shechinah* return during the Second Temple. For it says, '*Sing and be glad, O daughter of Zion! For behold, I am coming and I will dwell in your midst*' (*Zecharia 2:14*). The *Shechinah* was ready to dwell in the Second Temple as it had in the First Temple, had all the Jews willingly

---

24 From the time the Tabernacle was erected until the destruction of the Second Temple was close 900 years.

agreed to return [from the Babylonian exile]. But only some returned, while the majority—including the upper class and the Levites—remained in Babylonia, holding on to their homes and businesses.

"Perhaps this is what Solomon had in mind when he said, '*I am asleep, but My heart is awake (Shir Hashirim 5:2)*. He compared the Jews in exile to a person who is asleep. A person may be asleep, but his heart continues to beat. So too, even though the Jewish people were in exile, the spirit of prophecy was alive among them, [during the times of Chaggai, Zechariah and Malachi]. The verse continues, '*Hark, my Beloved knocks!*' suggesting God's call for the Jewish people to return to Eretz Yisrael. '*My head is drenched with dew*' refers to the *Shechinah* that withdrew from the Beis Hamikdash [and is waiting outside for the door to open, meanwhile becoming drenched with dew]. In the next verse the Jewish people answer, '*I have taken off My robe*'—[in other words: I have gone to bed, and I am too lazy to get up], indicating their reluctance to return. '*My Beloved sent forth His hand through the doorway*' alludes to the urgent calls to return to the Land, issued by Ezra, Nehemiah, and the other prophets. At last some of the people grudgingly agreed to go back, as it says, '*The men of Yehuda said, "The strength of the bearer is failing (Nechemiah 4:4)"*'.

"God retaliated for their reluctance to return by reducing the flow of Divine influence, and scaling down the intense Divine Presence that prevailed in the First Temple. A person receives only as much Divine influence as he is willing to receive. Had we greeted the God of our forefathers, wholeheartedly, we would have experienced the same miracles that happened to our forefathers in Egypt.

"Lamentably, when we recite such prayers as '*Bow at His holy mountain; bow at His footstool*' and '*Blessed are You Who restores His Presence to Zion,*' we are just mouthing words, like twittering birds. King of Khazar, you are right, we don't concentrate on what we are saying.

SACRIFICES

25. The Kuzari: "Please explain what I have read in the Torah about the sacrifices. I have trouble understanding the passage, '*My sacrifice, My food, for My fire, as My appeasing fragrance (Bamidbar 28:2)*'. Furthermore, how can sacrifices be called an '*offering to God*,' '*His food*,' and '*His pleasing fragrance*.'"

26. The Rabbi: "The phrase, '*for My fire*' clears up all difficulties. It shows that the 'sacrifice,' the 'food,' and the 'pleasing aroma' that is called for Me, are really '*for My fire*.' In other words, the sacrifices belong to the fire which was lit at My command. [After the fire consumed the portion placed on the Altar,] the *kohanim* eat the rest of the sacrifice. [The portion the *kohanim* eat is not God's food, and neither is the portion consumed by fire food for God. Rather it is food for the fire.] The underlying thought is that sacrifices lift the people to a spiritual height that enables the King to dwell among them metaphorically.

"Compare the idea of God dwelling among the Jewish people through the sacrifices to man's soul inhabiting his carnal body. A healthy person who is well-balanced, mentally and physically, is on a higher level than the animals. As long as he maintains his physical and mental stability, his intellect is his ruler, teacher, and guide. As soon as his inner harmony is disturbed, he loses his rationality. A fool may think his intellect thrives on food, drink, and fragrance, because he sees intelligent people need these things, and when they are starving they lose their common sense. Of course, the fool is wrong.

"[Obviously, the soul does not need food, drink or physical comforts.] But God, in His kindness allows a holy soul to attach itself to an earthly body, provided the body is prepared to receive a Divine soul. But when the bodily functions are in disarray, the body is unable to receive the Divine light, and it dissipates.

"God is too exalted to be affected by physical changes or deficiencies, [nevertheless if a person's constitution goes awry, the Soul will depart. The same applies to the Jewish nation as a whole. If they live by the Torah and bring the prescribed sacrifices, the *Shechinah* dwells among them. Otherwise it leaves them.] Therefore, the service that must be performed when bringing sacrifices—the incense, the recitation of psalms, the associated eating and drinking—must be performed in utmost purity and holiness. Thereby, they become what the Torah calls, '*the service of God,*' '*the food of God,*' and other such terms. '*The food of God,*' connotes that the sacrifice was offered the way God wanted it, by *kohanim* who are devout servants of God. When God "accepts the sacrifice", it means He honors the people by dwelling among them. Understand that God is far too exalted to find physical pleasure in food and drink. The sacrifices are for the spiritual benefit of those who bring them.

Analogy with the Organs of the Body

This can be compared to the human digestive system. Food is first digested in the stomach. From there it passes to the liver where impurities are filtered out. The refined substance provides nutrients for the heart where it is purified even more. The resulting pristine substance leaves the heart and nourishes the spirit. Thus, the food you eat sustains the heart, the mind, the brain, the digestive organs and other parts of the body. It reaches these organs by way of the blood that flows through your veins and arteries. The entire digestive system is designed so you can be guided by the reasoning soul, an almost angel-like entity. About angels it says, '*their dwelling is not with human beings*' *(Daniel 2:11)*. [When we say that the soul dwells inside the human body, we mean] that it guides the person. We don't suggest that it takes up space inside the body or savors food. It is exalted far above the physical world. [The soul, which is spiritual, becomes attached to the physical body through a gradual process.] The Divine soul [which is purely spiritual] attaches itself to the human spirit [which has a lower grade of spirituality]. The human spirit, in turn, connects with the natural life force [which is less spiritual than the human spirit]. The natural life force needs a place of attachment to the body, just as the flame is attached to the tip of the wick. The heart is compared to the wick and is nourished by the flow of blood. Since blood is produced by the digestive organs, it depends on the stomach, the liver, and the ducts that lead to these organs. The heart, in the same way, depends on the lungs, throat, nose, diaphragm, and the muscles that move the chest for breathing. Breathing regulates the temperature of the heart, because you inhale cool air and exhale warm air. To function properly, the heart also needs the removal of waste matter through bowel movements and urination. This gives you a summary of the functions of the bodily organs.

"Man must move in order to obtain the things he needs and to avoid harmful situations. He needs tools for bringing things to him or pushing things away from him. These tools are his hands and feet.

"Man needs 'advisers' to warn him of impending danger, notify him of good opportunities, record past experiences and to recommend the course of action he should follow. These 'advisers' are man's five senses and his memory. They are situated in his head and nourished by the heart which pumps the blood to the head.

"All the organs of the body are adapted to their functions, but they are controlled by the heart, where the soul first connects to the body. Human emotions [which are also spiritual in nature] reside in the brain, but emotions are stirred by the soul by way of the heart.

The Analogy to the Sanctuary

"The Divine life force reaches the Jewish people the same way. [The holy Ark, the focus of the Divine influence, is analogous to the heart.] As Joshua said, '*Through this [the Ark] will you know that the Living God is in your midst*' (*Yehoshua 3:10*). The fire on the Altar was lit by God when He chose the Jewish people as His nation, as a sign that He accepted their sacrifices. Fire is the most rarefied element in existence. [On the Altar] it makes contact with the more coarse earthly matter—the fat and smoke of the sacrifices, the incense, and the oils. Just as fire is fueled by oils and fats, so is man's warm life force nourished by the fine fatty globules in the blood.

[There were three fires in the Bais Hamikdash, each closer to the Ark than the next.] God commanded the construction of the [copper] Altar in the Courtyard of the Tabernacle, the [Golden] incense Altar inside the Sanctuary, and the Menorah. He then decreed laws for the offerings, the incense, the oil for the Menorah, and the anointing oil. The fire of the outer Altar for the burnt offerings was plainly visible; the fire of the golden incense Altar was a more delicate flame. The flame of the Menorah was even more ethereal, for it was meant to spread God's light of wisdom and knowledge. [These three fires represent the three stages of the human soul mentioned earlier: the Divine soul, the human spirit, and the natural life force. They parallel the three organs that connect with the soul: the liver, the heart and the brain]. The Table of showbreads was to bring down God's influence for material abundance and physical contentment. [Thus, the Table corresponds to the stomach.] That's why the Sages said: 'If you wish wisdom pray towards the south, [where the menorah was]; if you wish for riches, turn towards the north [where the table was].

"[The sacrifices, the showbreads, and the incense] were done for the sake of the Ark and the cherubim that stood on its Cover, [for the *Shechinah* manifested Itself between the two cherubim.] The Ark and the cherubim parallel the heart and the lungs that enclose the heart.

"All these furnishings needed accessories to service them, such as the laver and its base, wick tongs and ash scoops, dishes, spoons and shelving tubes, pots and forks, and so on. [These correspond to the auxiliary organs that help make the heart and the brain function properly: the mouth the nose, and the digestive and urinary tracts.] These furnishings also needed a place to house them—the

Tabernacle, its Tent, and its roof. [These compare to the skin, the flesh, and the bones.] The Courtyard and its vessels were needed as a protective enclosure. This portable structure accompanied the children of Israel on their wanderings through the wilderness. God chose the descendants of Levi to transport the Tabernacle because of their closeness to God, especially after the episode of the golden calf, where it says, '*All the Levites gathered around [Moshe]*' (*Shemos 32:26*). God chose Elazar, the most respected Levite, to carry the most precious and finest objects, as it says, '*The responsibility of Elazar son of Aaron the Kohen is the oil of illumination, the incense spices, the meal-offering and the anointment oil*' (*Bamidbar 4:16*). These were fuel for the pure and ethereal fire, the light of wisdom and knowledge, and the light of prophecy which became palpable in the *Urim VeTumim*.[25] [These correspond to the brain, the seat of the human intellect]

"The most distinguished of the Levite families—the family of Kehas—followed Elazar. They carried the vessels for the internal service, such as the Ark, the Table, the Menorah, the Altars and all the utensils pertaining to them. It says about them, '*Since they had the responsibility for the most sacred articles, they had to carry them on their shoulders*' (*Bamidbar 7:9*). [These match the internal organs.] The internal organs of the body do not have bones to move them, rather they have muscles attached to them allowing them to expand, contract and excrete.

"The Levite family of Gershon ranked below the Kehas group. They carried the pliable external furnishings of the Tabernacle. These included the Tabernacle's tapestries, the Tent of Meeting, its covering, the cover of *tachash* skins, and the drape at the entrance of the Tabernacle. [Gershon's responsibility matches the muscles that move the pliable parts of the body such as the mouth and the nose].

---

25 The *Urim Vetumim* was a slip of parchment containing the ineffable Name. This was inserted in the fold of the Breastplate. When the Kohen Gadol consulted the *Urim Vetumim*, the letters containing the answer would light up. With Divine inspiration the High Priest would then be able to combine the letters to spell out the answer.

"The Merari family ranked below the Gershon group. They were in charge of carrying the rigid vessels: the hooks, beams, bars, pillars, and sockets. The task of the Gershon and Merari families was made easier because they were given wagons. As it says, '*Two wagons . . . for the descendants of Gershon . . . and four wagons . . . for the descendants of Merari*' (*Bamidbar 7:7,8*). [The beams and pillars correspond to the legs and the hands.]

"All this was arranged and put in order by Divine wisdom. I do not say—God forbid—that my explanation is the underlying thought of the sacrificial service. The intention behind it is really far more wondrous and beyond human understanding. The sacrificial service is part of God's Torah, and a person who accepts the Torah completely without trying to justify it with his intellect is greater than one who applies logic and tries to find reasons [for the commandments]. However, if you are not on that high level and want to investigate the reasons for the commandments, accept this explanation, rather than following spurious speculations which take you away from the path of the Torah."

ISRAEL, THE HEART OF MANKIND

27. The Kuzari: "Rabbi, the analogies you drew [between the sacrifices and the human body] are brilliant. But I have yet to hear the analogy to the head and its sensory organs. And what about the anointing oil? You haven't given an analogy for that either."

28. The Rabbi: "The source of wisdom resides in the Ark which is compared to the heart; for the source of all wisdom is the Ten Commandments and the Torah, both of which lay in the ark, as it says, '*Take this Torah scroll and place it to the side of the Ark of God's covenant*' (*Devarim 31:26*). Two wisdoms emanated from them: the wisdom of the Torah [i.e., the knowledge of the mitzvos] which is taught by the *kohanim*, and the wisdom of prophecy which was attained by the prophets. The *kohanim* and the prophets were the advisers who admonished and cautioned the people. They, therefore, represent the 'head' of the Jewish nation."

29. The Kuzari: "[Since the Ark has vanished, and prophecy has ended,] you are today a body without a head and without a heart!"

30. The Rabbi: "What you say is quite true! We are not even a body; we are just scattered bones, like the 'dry bones' Ezekiel saw in his vision. Even so, King of Khazar, these bones have a trace of life left in them, since they once contained the head, heart, life force, spirit and soul. Therefore, they are better than the unbroken bodies [of other nations] whose head, eyes and ears, and other parts are made of stone and plaster. These bodies never had the spirit of life in them, and there is no chance they ever will. They are nothing but hulks that look human, but are not."

31. The Kuzari: "You are right."

32. The Rabbi: "The 'dead' nations that have tried to copy the 'living' nation, have only been able to mimic them superficially. They built shrines for their god, but no sign of godliness appeared in them. They have lived as ascetics in order to achieve prophecy, but it never came. They became corrupt, angered God and rebelled against Him, but no fire ever came down from heaven to punish them. Nor have they suffered any sudden plague telling them that their punishment came from God. As result of their transgressions, their 'heart' [which represents, their house of worship] was destroyed. [Even though their heart was destroyed] their prosperity did not go downhill. Rather, changes in their welfare are due to political factors, such as demographics, military strength, and unity or divisiveness.

"By contrast, when our 'heart'—meaning our Temple—was destroyed, we, too, were destroyed. And when our Temple will be restored, we too, will be restored, no matter the circumstance. For our Leader, King, and Ruler, Who strengthens us in our dispersion and exile, is the Living God."

33. The Kuzari: "True. It is unthinkable that any nation could be sent into a harsh exile like yours without adopting the culture and religion of the oppressor nation, especially after such a long time. In fact there were many nations who were exiled after the Jews and they did not retain their identity; for example the Edomites and Moabites etc."

34. The Rabbi: "Though I said earlier [that we are just scattered bones], this does not mean we are no longer alive. [Even though the Ark and prophecy are gone], we are still connected to Divinity through the laws of the Torah that God instituted as links between us. Circumcision is one example, about which it says, '*My covenant shall be in your flesh for an everlasting covenant*' (*Bereishis 17:13*). Another such law is the Sabbath, about which it says, '*It is a sign between Me and you for your generations*' (*Shemos 31:13*). On top of that there is the covenant that God made with our forefathers, and the covenant He made with us both at Mount Sinai, and the Plains of Moab. This covenant carries with it the promise of reward and punishment as recorded in the Torah section, '*When you will have children . . .*' (*Devarim 4:25-40*) in the section, '*When all these things will come upon you,*' (*Devarim 30:1-10*) in the song of *Haazinu* (Devarim 32:1-43), and in other places.

"We are not really dead, but rather like a sick man who is withering away. After the doctors gave up hope, he clings to the hope of a miraculous cure. That is what is meant by the passage, '*Can these bones live again*' (*Yechezkel 37:3*)? [The imagery of seeing the Jewish people as a sick man is echoed in the verses], '*Behold, My servant [the Jewish people] will succeed,*' (*Yeshayah 52:13—53:12*) especially in the passages, '*He has neither form nor grandeur, a man of suffering, familiar with disease, . . . one from whom we would hide our faces . . . He was despised, and we had no regard for him*'. Because of the sick person's emaciated look, people turn away from him, much like a squeamish person will turn away from dirty things.

35. The Kuzari: "But how can you say the sick man in this passage refers to the Jewish people? [The Jewish people we know, are punished for their own sins not the sins of others.] And the aforementioned verse continues, '*but it was our sickness he was bearing and our suffering he carried; we thought that he was afflicted and punished by God [for his own sins]. But in truth he was pained because of our sins and oppressed because of our misdeeds' (Yeshayah 53:4).*"

36. The Rabbi: "Israel among the nations is like the heart among the organs of the body. The heart is immediately affected by the condition of the other organs; if they are ailing, it ails; if they are well, it is well. You might say, the heart is the sickest organ in the body, and at the same time, the healthiest."

37. The Kuzari: "Please elaborate."

38. The Rabbi: "The heart is susceptible to illness at all times because it is continually tormented by worry, grief, fear, grudge, hate, desire, and alarm. Its disposition changes from one moment to the next. It is sensitive to changes in the weather, bad food or drink, movement and exertion, sleep or the lack of it. The other organs remain at ease and are not affected by these factors."

39. The Kuzari: "I can see how the heart is the sickest of all organs. But please explain: in what way is it also the healthiest?"

40. The Rabbi: "Is it possible for the heart to function when it is stricken by an abscess, a tumor, a blister, a wound, a heart attack, or coronary weakness, as other organs can?"

41. The Kuzari: "Any of these disorders would be fatal. The heart is an extremely sensitive organ. Because of the purified blood that circulates through the heart, it detects the slightest abnormality and fights it off before it does irreparable damage. By contrast, other organs lack this acute sensitivity. That's why their sickness remains unnoticed and is allowed to spread to the point where it becomes life-threatening."

42. The Rabbi: "It is the heart's sensitivity that makes it vulnerable to so many sicknesses, but, it is this same sensitivity that enables it to wipe out any germs before they have a chance to gain control."

43. The Kuzari: "Yes."

44. The Rabbi: "The Divine influence relates to us as the soul relates to the heart. [Just as the soul initially connects with the heart and then spreads to the rest of the body, so too, God's influence first connects with the Jewish people and then spreads to the rest of the world]. And so it says, '*You alone have I singled out of all the families of the earth—that is why I will call you to account for all your sins*' (*Amos* 3:2). This corresponds to the malady of the heart in our analogy [because the Jewish people are punished immediately for their sins].

"The analogy of the heart being the healthiest of all organs can be explained by the prayer formulated by the Sages, 'He forgives the sins of His nation; He removes sins one by one.' God does not allow our sins to accumulate to the extent where they cause complete destruction. But in contrast He allowed the sins of the Emorites to pile up, as God said to Avraham, '*The fourth generation will return [to the Land], for the sins of the Emorites will not be full until then*' (*Bereishis* 15:16). God left the Emorites alone until the sickness of their sins became malignant and killed them.

"Just as the heart's healthful condition makes it ideal for the soul to attach itself, so does the Divine influence attach Itself to the Jewish people because of their innate righteousness. But [despite the heart's inherent soundness] it can become infected by disorders of the liver which is the source of anger, the stomach [which are caused by gluttony], or the male organ [through excessive lust]. The same way, the Jewish people becomes corrupted by the life style of the other nations, as it says, '*They mingled with the nations and learned their ways*' (*Tehillim* 106:35).

"In light of that, it is not implausible for the nations to say, '*It was our sickness that he was bearing.*' We suffer the bitter exile, [because of the sins of the nations] while the rest of the world enjoys tranquility. [With our suffering we cleanse the sins of the world].

The calamities that befall us are meant to make us submissive, and to cleanse us. When we are free of all impurities, the Divine influence can attach Itself to us and to the entire world.

"The physical elements appeared gradually: first there were minerals, then came the plants, animals, and man, and finally, the noblest of all mankind, [the Jewish people]. The entire process was brought into being for the sake of this chosen nation, so that the Divine influence could attach Itself to it. This chosen nation in turn exists for the sake of the elite, the devout ones. This progression [from mankind to Israel to the devout] is reflected in the prayer [we say on Rosh Hashana and Yom Kippur]: 'Instill Your awe upon all Your works,' followed by, 'Grant honor to Your nation,' and then, 'The righteous will see and be glad.' Because the righteous are the most treasured of the treasured nation."

45. The Kuzari: "Your analogy describing the Jewish people as the heart of mankind is proper. [But if you are special,] I would expect to see more ascetics engaged in contemplating God among you than among other religions."

46. The Rabbi: "Didn't we agree that one cannot draw close to God except by the performance of His commandments? You can not get close to God just by being submissive."

RATIONAL LAWS AND DIVINE COMMANDMENTS

47. The Kuzari: Yes, righteousness to your fellowman combined with a humble spirit will bring you close to God. In fact, I've even found this in your Torah, as it says, *'What does God require of you: Only to do justice, and to love goodness, and to walk modestly with your God' (Michah* 6:8) and many other passages like this."

48. The Rabbi: "These and similar [rules of ethics] are rational laws, [which you yourself can figure out]. They are the essentials that pave the way to the Divine Torah. No society can function without a code of behavior. Even a gang of robbers cannot exist unless they have a system of justice; without it, their conspiracy falls apart.

"[Let me explain why the prophet Michah seems to stress rational laws, such as acting fairly and being humble.]

"Israel rebelled against God, ignoring the rules of social order without which society cannot survive, just as a person cannot exist without eating, drinking, moving and resting. [While neglecting the rational laws,] they concentrated on bringing sacrifices and observing other Divinely ordained laws, [like *sukkah, shofar, tefillin, tzitzit*]. The prophet [Michah] admonished them, saying: Obey the fundamental laws of ethics observed even by the most primitive societies, such as maintaining justice, helping the underprivileged, and thanking God for His bounty. You cannot properly fulfill the Divinely ordained laws unless you first observe the basic rational laws of ethics.

"The Divinely ordained laws were given to us in addition to the basic rational laws. And it is through these God-given laws that the Jewish people received the advantage of the Divine influence.

"But [once they abandoned the rational laws] they could not understand why they had to observe all these laws. Neither could they grasp how God's glory once dwelled among them, how the fire of God once came down on their sacrifices, how their ancestors could hear God's words, or how the miracles their ancestors experienced took place—things no one could believe if they were not validated by the irrefutable evidence of a multitude of eye witnesses.

"And so the prophet [Michah] told them, '*What does God require of you*' *(Michah 6:8)*, and, '*Add your burnt offerings to your peace offerings and eat their meat*' *(Yirmeyah 7:21)* [Meaning: You may as well eat the meat of the burnt offerings though the law requires they be completely burned. They are not acceptable to God anyway (Rashi).] The prophet did not mean that all God requires from a Jew is justice and kindness, while ignoring circumcision, the laws of Sabbath and Passover, and other laws. Can you expect a Jew who scorns the God-given commandments to come close to God?"

49. The Kuzari: "Of course not. That is unthinkable as you have explained. But, the philosophers believe that a person can become a holy man no matter what religion he follows. If we accept their view, we come to depend on logical inferences, reasoning, and generalizations. Every person would establish a religion based on his own speculations which would be pointless."

The Torah Does Not Demand Asceticism

50. The Rabbi: "The Torah does not ask you to become a self-denying recluse. Instead, follow the middle road, giving both body and spirit their due, without favoring one at the expense of the other. A person who overindulges in physical pleasures diminishes his thinking power, and vice versa. A person who has an excessive hunger for power represses his good qualities.

"Serving God by taking on fasts is not recommended for a person who is frail. Instead of fasting, he should pamper his body. Nor is living in poverty a pious act for a person who makes an honest living and whose business affairs do not interfere with his Torah studies and good deeds. Certainly, if he has a family to support and wants to earn money for charity, then pursuing wealth should be encouraged.

"Our Torah laws are evenly balanced between those that evoke awe, and those that inspire love and joy. You can draw close to God by both of these approaches. Your submissiveness on fast days will not bring you closer to God than your joy on the Sabbath and festivals if your joy is sparked by a wholehearted intent to fulfill God's command. Just as prayer requires thought and intent, so does the joy of performing a commandment or studying the Torah require thought and intent. Find joy in the fact that God selected you to serve Him. This will arouse in you a love for the One Who gave these commandments, and gratitude for how good He has been to you. Feel as if you were a guest in His house, invited to enjoy His table and His favors; thereby you will thank Him privately and publicly. If your joy moves you to sing and dance, that too, is a form of worship that brings you closer to God.

"The Torah did not leave it to people to decide when to fast and when to rejoice, because man is unable to determine how to keep his body and soul on the right track. He can not know how much rest and exertion is recommended, how long the land should produce before it must remain fallow during the Sabbatical and the Jubilee years, or that the produce should be tithed. That's why God decreed that the Sabbath and the festivals should be observed, and that the land should rest [during the seventh year of the *shemittah* cycle].

"All these ordinances are designed as a remembrance of the Exodus and of Creation. These two events share a common denominator in that both were accomplished by God's will and did not happen by chance.

"That's why the Torah says, '*You might inquire about times long past, going back to the time that God created man on earth . . . Has any nation ever heard God speaking out of fire, as you have, and survived? Or has any god ever miraculously come to take one nation out of another nation?*' (Devarim 4:32-34).

"By keeping Shabbos we acknowledge that God created the universe. If you observe Shabbos because the work of creation was completed on it, you are testifying thereby that the world was created out of nothing. When you believe in Creation, you automatically declare your belief in the Creator. A person who does not keep Shabbos is beset by doubt about the origin of the universe, and his faith in God is flawed. In fact the joy of Shabbos brings you closer to the Creator than self-denial and abstinence.

"[Self-denial is not the right approach, as we see from the fact that] the Divine influence attached Itself to Avraham and afterwards to the multitude of His treasured nation, [and they were not hermits]. In the Holy Land the Divine influence gradually increased. God watched over Yaakov's children and none were lost [through intermarriage or assimilation]. God settled them in the best of all places [in Goshen which is the most fertile part of Egypt] where He caused them to multiply and increase in amazing num-

bers. He ultimately took them out of Egypt bringing them to the
land that was a suitable home for His treasured nation.

God Loves Us Because of our Forefathers

"God is called 'God of Avraham,' and 'God of Yitzchok,' just as He
is known as, 'He Who resides between the cherubim,' and 'He Who
dwells in Zion,' and 'He Who dwells in Jerusalem'. The verses compare our forefathers to the heavens because the Divine light was apparent in the forefathers just as it is apparent in the heavens.
[Although God's light radiates all over,] it reaches only those who
are tuned to its 'wavelength' [i.e., the forefathers]. This outpouring of Divine light is called 'God's love.' We believe that God's love
came down to us by way of the forefathers. We thankfully express
this in the [Ahava Rabbah] prayer that opens with the words, 'With
an abundant love have You loved us . . . For the sake of our forefathers who trusted in You. . . may You be equally gracious to us
and teach us.' This prayer makes us aware that His love originated
from Him as a favor, not as reward for anything we did.

"By way of illustration, we know that animals did not create
themselves, but were created [at God's initiative], by God Who selected the suitable raw material. Similarly, it was God Who took us
out of Egypt, to be His chosen nation, and to be our King, [as a
favor, not in return for anything we did]. This idea is mentioned in
several places, such as, 'I am God your Lord, Who brought you out of
Egypt to be your God'(Bamidbar 15:41) and, 'Israel, in whom I take
glory' (Yeshayah 49:3)".

ISRAEL, A SOURCE OF GLORY FOR GOD

51. The Kuzari: "The poetic language of the last verse seems to
downgrade God by suggesting that He derives glory from human
beings."

52. The Rabbi: "Would it sound better if the verse had said that God derives glory from the creation of the sun?"

53. The Kuzari: "Yes, because of the sun's great power. The sun comes second only to God in the impact it has on the world. The sun determines night and day, and it causes the seasons of the year. Minerals, plants, and living creatures exist because of it, and it is only through the sun's bright light that you are able to see. Why then, should people not consider the sun a source of glory for its Maker?"

54. The Rabbi: "Isn't the light of the intellect more ethereal and sublime than the visible light [of the sun]? Before the Jewish nation appeared on the scene, all nations were blind to the truth except for select individuals in each generation. One of those nations believed there was no Creator. They believed it was impossible for the world or living creatures to be created, and the world always was as it is today with no Creator and no beginning. Another nation worshipped the spheres because they believed that the heavenly spheres always existed, and they created everything else. Still others worshiped fire because they foolishly thought that, [the sun was a ball of fire] and fire was the source of all the wondrous and massive forces in the world. They went so far as to say that the human soul is a form of fire. Another nation worshiped such things as the sun, moon, stars, and the signs of the zodiac, while yet another worshiped their kings and wise men. All these nations agreed that no miracles could ever occur.

"[The nations drifted in darkness] until the days of the philosophers. Their keen analysis led them to the conclusion that there is a Prime Cause unlike everything else in the world. However, they reasoned that the Prime Cause because it was so exalted does not occupy itself with this world, much less with individuals.

"[The rejection of the Divine Creator] continued until the Jewish people were purified. Once they were worthy to have the Divine light shine on them, and to have awesome miracles performed for them, they saw that the world has a Ruler and a

Guardian, Who is a Creator and Who regulates the course of nature. He knows everything that happens—from the trivial to the momentous—and He rewards good and punishes evil. The Jewish nation was destined to become the guiding light for all the people of the world. The religions that were spin-offs of Judaism [such as Christianity and Islam] could not divorce themselves from the principles of Judaism, so that today the entire world acknowledges that God created the universe. They see the Jewish people and their history—both in triumph and defeat—as proof of this."

55. The Kuzari: "The fact that Israel is the guiding light for the people of the world is the greatest glory for God. This is supported by the verses *'You split the sea before them to make Yourself eternal renown' (Yeshayah 63:12); 'You took Your people out of the land of Egypt with a strong hand and gained Yourself renown as of this day' (Daniel 9:15)*, and *'To make you supreme over all the nations that He made, for praise, for renown, and for splendor'" (Devarim 26:19)*.

56. The Rabbi: "[The light of the Jewish people shines brighter than the sun. Let me prove it to you.] Look how highly David praises the Torah. He begins by speaking about the sun, *'The heavens declare the glory of God' (Tehillim 19)*. He then describes the sun's pervasive light, its radiance, its straight course, and its beauty. In the next verse he says, *'God's Torah is perfect, restoring the soul,'* and so on *(Tehillim 19:8)*. It is as if he were saying: Don't be overwhelmed by the marvels of the sun. The Torah is even brighter, more encompassing, more acclaimed, more beneficial and exalted.

"But if not for the Jews, there would be no Torah. [So you see, since the Jewish people are greater than the Torah, and the Torah is brighter than the sun, it follows that the light of the Jewish people outshines the sun.] They did not attain their eminence because of Moshe's merit; on the contrary, Moshe derived his greatness from the merit of the Jewish people. God's love could not flow down on a community without the offspring of Avraham, Yitzchok, and Yaakov present in it. God merely chose Moshe as the agent to bring His great goodness to them. That's why we are not called the 'nation of Moshe's but rather 'the nation of God,' as it says, '*These are the people of God*' *(Yechezkel 36:20), and '*The people of the God of Avraham*' *(Tehillim 47:10).*

Keeping the Mitzvos is What Counts

[Addressing the Kuzari's earlier remark about the numerous ascetics and monks among the other religions, the Rabbi returns to that subject.]

"A person cannot prove that he is truly devout by using flowery phrases, raising his eyebrows, closing his eyes during prayer, offering many supplications, or by sanctimonious talk without deeds to back it up. Deeds that are difficult to perform, yet are done with dedication and love are what count. One example is making a pilgrimage to the Temple in Jerusalem three times a year [on the pilgrimage festivals]. In spite of the great expense and hardship these journeys entail, the person looks forward to them with great joy. Other examples of cumbersome deeds that a Jew does joyfully are: disbursing the first tithe to the Levites, bringing the second tithe to Jerusalem, and giving the 'poor man's tithe.' He brings the required festival offerings, leaves the land fallow during the Sabbatical and Jubilee years, incurs expenses in order to celebrate the Sabbath and festivals, and refrains from working on those days. He offers his first-fruits, his firstborn, the first of his wool shearings, the first of his dough, and other priestly gifts. He fulfills his vows and free-will offerings, brings sacrifices for intentional and unintentional sins, makes his peace offerings, and discharges sacrificial obligations due because of personal contamination, ritual defilement, *tzoraas*, childbirth, or other things. Observance of these and similar commandments is the only proof of genuine piety— [not withdrawal from the world].

"All these laws were ordained by God. They are not human inventions. A human being could not come up with a code containing as many intricate details as this, without miscalculating. Can anyone, while yet in the wilderness, estimate the exact population of the people at the time of their entry into the land forty years later? Could anyone forecast the fertility of Canaan as regards vegetable and animal production? God considered the future numbers of the Levites and ordained these assessments while the Jews were still in the wilderness. God knew then, that if the Jewish people maintained the prescribed amounts [of gifts to the *kohanim* and the Levites], the nation would remain prosperous while the Levites would also thrive. When Eretz Yisrael was first apportioned to each family God made sure no tribe or family would become destitute, through the Divine command that in the Jubilee year all property revert back to the original owners. The specifications of these laws alone could fill an entire library. Examine them carefully and you will recognize that they are not of human origin, but were designed by the Praised and Exalted One. '*He did not do so for any other people; of such rules they know nothing*' *(Tehillim 1:20)*. This code of laws [as it relates to the service of the Beis Hamikdash] was in force for close to 1500 years. Had the Jewish people stayed on the right path, they would have remained in their land forever."

57. The Kuzari: "[It is easier for you] now that you live in exile, because you are freed of all these laws. Who could possibly observe all those rules [that applied when they were in Eretz Yisrael]?"

PUNISHMENT FOR TRANSGRESSIONS

58. The Rabbi: "The nation that is mindful of the presence of the *Shechinah*, who punished immediately for transgressions and rewards good deeds can observe these rules. As Joshua said [to the people in his final oration], '*You will not be able to serve God, for He is a holy God. He is a jealous God; He will not forgive your transgressions and your sins*' *(Yehoshua 24:19)*. Joshua said this, even though his community was made up of devout people, who were so conscientious no one violated the ban on taking from the spoils of Jericho, except for Achan. Nevertheless, God's punishment [to the entire community] came swiftly, [and in the battle for the city of Ai that followed, thirty-six men were lost]. Similarly Miriam was punished immediately with leprosy [for speaking against Moshe], Nadav and Avihu were punished [for offering an unauthorized fire], and Uzza and the people of Bet Shemesh, for showing disrespect toward the Ark.

"A sign that the *Shechinah* rested among the Jewish people was that God's displeasure with minor sins showed up immediately [as a divinely inspired leprous *tzaraas* mark] on the walls of their houses or on their garments; and when their sins mounted, their bodies broke out with varying degrees of this *tzaraas* disease. The *kohanim* were experts in diagnosing this Divinely inflicted sickness, whose lesions were due to natural causes and which were Divine punishment for deplorable conduct. This required an extraordinary amount of proficiency. They sometimes isolated the patient for one or two weeks, as they did with Miriam. Therefore the creator cautioned, '*Be careful with regard to leprous signs and carefully keep [the rules]. Be very careful to do all that the Levitical priests decide for you, as I have commanded them*'" (Devarim 24:8).

Explanation of Tzaraas

59. The Kuzari: "Do you know any rational explanation for the *tzaraas* affliction?"

60. The Rabbi: "You cannot compare our intellect to the infinitely great Divine Wisdom. Therefore, we shouldn't even try to fathom the reasons for these lofty concepts. But, after asking God's forgiveness, and stating in advance that my explanation is not necessarily true, I will say that both *tzaraas* and the impurity that results from abnormal discharges are related to the impurity that governs a dead body. Death is the total lack of spirituality, and a limb afflicted with *tzaraas* is like a dead body in this regard. An abnormal discharge of semen also represents death, because the semen had potential life making force.

"Since the absence of spirituality [from *tzaraas* and discharges] is very subtle, it can only be detected by sensitive souls who attempt to become close to God and who experience prophetic visions. Some saintly people feel sluggish when they have not purified themselves from their discharges [by immersing in a *mikveh*]. Saintly people [in an impure condition] can damage delicate objects by their touch, such as pearls [which lose their gloss] and wine [which turns sour]. Most of us have a weird feeling when we come close to a cemetery, and we are unnerved when we enter a house where a dead person has been. A coarse person is not affected by any of this.

"We see the same in intellectual matters. A person who tries to improve himself by studying metaphysics or by praying will find that heavy foods and overeating slow him down. Mingling with women, scorners, or listening to love songs or silly tunes hampers his progress."

61. The Kuzari: "This clarifies why the discharge of semen can impart spiritual impurity, even though semen creates life, whereas urine and feces do not impart impurity even though they have a foul odor and greater bulk. But I still don't understand *tzaraas* of houses and clothing."

62. The Rabbi: "The *Shechinah* dwelled among the Jewish people like a soul residing in a person's body. It introduced a Divine life force and radiance in their bodies, personalities, and homes. When this Divine life force withdrew, their intelligence lapsed into foolishness, their bodies wilted, and their beauty faded away. You could tell when the *Shechinah* had left a person.

"Similarly, when sudden fear takes a person's breath away, his body is unsettled. Women and children—because of their impressionable nature—may develop black or green marks [caused by panic] from being out alone at night. People say these marks are the work of demons. Sometimes serious physical and mental disorders are caused by such fears, or from seeing dead people or murder victims. [The same way, when the Divine force departs, it causes the marks of *tzaraas* to appear in the person, in his house or in his clothing.]"

THE IMPORTANCE OF SCIENCE

63. The Kuzari: "Unlike other religions, your Torah covers all aspects of the sciences."

64. The Rabbi: "The members of the Sanhedrin—[the highest court of seventy-one sages]—were required to be accomplished [not only in Torah learning but] in all branches of wisdom—they had to know the natural sciences as well as astrology, grammar, foreign languages even black magic. A high standard of learning was the norm among the people, and seventy competent scholars were available at all times, when one sage died, another of the same caliber was ready to take over.

"How could it be otherwise? Knowledge of all the sciences is needed to apply the laws of the Torah. You must know botany not to plant your field with mixed seeds [*kilayim*], to observe the Sabbatical year and the law of *orlah* which forbids fruits from the first three years of a newly planted tree. You need to identify the different kinds of plants and their varieties, so that each plant should remain the way it was created without being mixed with another species. It takes great expertise to know whether the barley called *kondros* is really barley, and whether rye is a type of wheat, and whether the cabbage called *korbator* is really a type of cabbage. You must know the strength of the roots of a given plant, how far they spread in the ground, and whether the roots last until the next season, in order to know how far apart two different species must be spaced, and how much time you must wait after harvesting one species before planting another in the same field.

"For the same reason you must identify the various species of animals, [because the prohibition of mixing species applies also to animals. In order to determine which animals are *trief*]²⁶ you have to determine which animals give off venom and which do not. You must know which wounds or diseases render an animal *tereifah*. These laws are more complex than anything Aristotle wrote about mortal wounds to deter people from eating carrion. Only a small fraction of the knowledge of the Sages has come down to us, but even that, fills us with awe of the breadth and depth of their wisdom.

"[You have to be proficient in medicine] to know which blemishes disqualify a *kohen* from serving in the Temple, and which blemishes render an animal unfit to be brought as a sacrifice.

"You need to identify the different discharges and the laws of *niddah*. No one could grasp the fine points of these matters without help from God.

Why We Need Astronomy

"Astronomy enables us to calculate the conjunction of the moon and the sun, which forms the basis of the Jewish calendar. This science is ingrained in our consciousness. We may be poor materially, but intellectually we are very wealthy. We are snubbed by the nations because of our small number and lowly status in exile; but we are united because of the Torah—particularly the calculation of the Jewish calendar. It fuses us into one nation. [Wherever there are Jews, they celebrate the holy days according to the Jewish calendar.]

"One of the most amazing things about the Jewish calendar is the calculation of the lunar month [which is 29 days, 12 hours, and 793/1080 of an hour or 29.53059 days]. This was handed down to us by the family of David. This figure has remained unchanged for thousands of years because it is based on prophetic tradition.²⁷

---

²⁶ Any animal suffering from a condition that can cause it to die is forbidden even if it has been ritually slaughtered.

²⁷ According to National Aeronautics and Space Agency, the length of the lunar month is 29.503588 days. Thus, the difference between this figure and the figure of 29.53059 handed down from David is .000002, or two millionth of a day. (Pathways to the Torah, by Arachim).

"By contrast, other calendars had to be adjusted every century. If the calculations of the Sages were even slightly off, over the centuries, an error of a fraction of a second would add up to days and cause a serious discrepancy between the calculated *molad* and the actual sighting of the new moon, [but this did not happen]. [Just as the Sages knew how to calculate the lunar month], they undoubtedly knew how to figure the length of the solar year and the orbits of the planets."

The Importance of Music

"Music was rated so highly in our nation that it was assigned exclusively to our spiritual leaders, the Levites. They sang and played various instruments in the Holy Temple at every important function. The Levites were sustained by the tithes contributed by the people, so they did not need to earn a livelihood. Their sole occupation was [to be Torah teachers] and to study music. Music is a highly esteemed art, although it is abused by uncultured musicians. The first to introduce the concept of art and music in Jewry were David and Samuel."

65. The Kuzari: "Music reached its perfection in the Holy Temple. It touched the soul of the people, elevating them to such heights that it changed their very nature. You cannot compare today's music with the music of those days. Music is no longer a respectable occupation. Today's musicians are worthless fellows and derelicts. Music has lost its former greatness, just as the Jewish people have lost their bygone prominence."

66. The Rabbi: "[Music is not the only art that has declined.] Helped by God and with his innate intellectual prowess Solomon mastered all fields of knowledge. Scholars from all over the world— as far as India—flocked to him to copy his wisdom for their own use. The roots of all secular knowledge originated with us. From us it passed to the Chaladeans [i.e. the Babylonians, after the destruction of the First Temple], then to the Persians and Medians, then to the Greeks, and finally to the Romans. With the passing years and the numerous translations of the Hebrew texts, people forgot that this knowledge originated with the Jews, thinking it came from the Greeks and Romans. [Besides, the translators were unable to capture the true meaning of the Hebrew texts,] because the Hebrew language can convey abstract and scientific concepts far better than any other language can."

THE SUPERIORITY OF THE HEBREW LANGUAGE

67. The Kuzari: "Is Hebrew superior to Arabic? Arabic has a richer vocabulary and offers more synonyms than Hebrew."

68. The Rabbi: "Hebrew has suffered the same fate as the Jews who speak it, declining because the Jews went into decline. [As the Jews adopted the language of the countries of their exile, they gradually forgot Hebrew.] But Hebrew is the most important of all languages, from a historical and a logical point of view.

"Historically, Hebrew is the language in which God spoke to Adam and Eve, and in which they talked to each other. The roots of their names prove this: *Adam* is derived from *adamah* (earth); *ishah* (woman) from *ish* (man); *Chavah* (Eve) from *chai* (life); *Cain* from *kanisi* (I have acquired); *Shes* from *shas* (granted); *Noach* from *yenachameinu* (He will bring us relief).

"Furthermore the Torah [given by God is written in Hebrew]. The Hebrew language was handed through the generations from Ever who received it from Noach, who received it from Adam. It is called *Ivris* [Hebrew] because it was Ever's language. Ever was the only one that continued to speak Hebrew after the Generation of Dispersion when all the languages were confused.

"Avraham spoke Aramaic in Ur Kasdim, because Aramaic was the language of the Chaldeans, [thus it was his native tongue]. He spoke Hebrew when discussing sacred topics, but Aramaic was his vernacular. Yishmael brought Hebrew to the Arab countries where it blended with Arabic. As a result, the three languages—Aramaic, Arabic and Hebrew—have many similarities in their vocabularies, conjugations, and grammar. Hebrew being the most refined.

"Hebrew is superior because it was used by the Jewish people. They needed beautiful metaphors [in their orations], especially when prophecy flourished, [and prophets needed a lucid language] to express God's will. They also needed a language that would fit the rhythms of melodies for songs and praises. Jewish leaders such as Moshe, Joshua, David and Solomon did not lack lyrical phrases when they made speeches. They did not need to borrow foreign idioms as we do today. The Torah, when describing the Tabernacle, priestly apron, and breastplate always finds the most suitable word for everything, and the Torah's stories are beautifully structured. The Torah was able to provide Hebrew names for all nations, birds, and gems. The Hebrew language was beautiful enough for David to compose his psalms, for Job to voice his protestations and his debates with his friends, for Isaiah to deliver his words of reproof and consolation, and so on."

Poetry and Song

69. The Kuzari: "You have shown that Hebrew is as rich a language as the others. But in what respect is it superior? The other languages lend themselves better to rhyme and rhythm in poetry and song."

70. The Rabbi: "A person does not speak in poetic patterns. For example, you can sing, *'Praise God for He is good' (Tehillim 136)* and *'To Him Who alone performs great wonders'* [although the two segments of the verse do not have the same number of syllables]. However, you can do that only with free verse, not with the metrical form of poetry. The Jewish Sages did not compose songs that follow a strict meter. In their writings they wanted to create something higher and more useful."

71. The Kuzari: "And what is that?"

72. The Rabbi: "The purpose of language is to communicate the thoughts of the soul of the speaker to the soul of the listener. This can be achieved best only if speaker and listener are facing each other. The spoken word is better than the written word; or, as the saying goes, 'Better to learn from the *mouth* of sages than from their *books*.' A speaker will pause when a pause is called for, and will continue to speak when the sentences flow into each other. Occasionally, he will modulate his voice for greater emphasis. He can also use body language—eye movements and mouth gestures—to suggest astonishment and question, to relate statistical facts, to express hope, fear, or submission. A raised eyebrow, a condescending smirk, or a raised hand convey the speaker's anger, desire, submissiveness or arrogance much better than lengthy explanations.

"The little we have left of our language—which was created by God—contains certain subtle marks designed to help you understand the text. These marks take the place of the speaker's gestures which you see when you are facing him. These are the cantillation marks [*ta'amei hamikra* or *trop*] that we use to read our holy books. They tell you where to pause and where to continue reading; they separate the question from the answer, the subject from the predicate, command from request and that which is said quickly from that which is said slowly. It would take many books to treat this subject comprehensively.

"A speaker who wants to convey his ideas effectively will stay away from formal poetry, because such poetry can be recited only one way. With measured poetry he will connect where he should stop and stop where he should continue."

73. The Kuzari: "You are right. The rhythmic sound of formal poetry should give way to a better understanding of the text. The harmonic sound of formal poetry pleases the ear, but the traditional cantillation signs make the meaning clear."

[Paragraphs 74 to 80 deal with complex grammatical issues and have been omitted.]

81. The Kuzari: "Through your expositions I have come to love the Hebrew language. Now I'd like you to explain to me what you understand a servant of God to be. Afterward I will ask about your arguments against the Karaites. Then I will ask you about the fundamentals of Jewish beliefs and faith. Finally I will ask you what you have left of the body of knowledge [your Sages possessed.]"

This concludes Part Two, with the help of God.

GLOSSARY

AVRAHAM - Abraham
BEIS HAMIKDASH - Holy Temple
BERACHA pl. *BERACHOS* - blessing
EISAV - Esau
ERETZ YISRAEL - The Land of Israel
GAN EDEN - The Garden of Eden
GEMARA - Talmud
HASHEM - God
KESUVAH - marriage contract
KOHEN pl. *KOHANIM* - Priests, descendants of Aaron
LULAV - palm branch take on Sukkos
MIKVEH - ritual immersion pool
MILAH - circumcision
MISHNAH - compilation of the oral tradition; it also refers to one paragraph of this *MISHNAH*
MITZVAH pl. *MITZVOS* - commandment
MOSHE - Moses
NIDDAH - menstruant woman
ROSH CHODESH - The begining of the Jewish month
SANHEDRIN - Jewish court
SHECHNIAH - The Divine Presence
SHMITTAH - the sabbatical year when work in the field as prohibited
SHABBOS - The day of rest - Saturday
SHOFAR - Ram's horn blown on Rosh Hashana
SUKKAH - hut used on the Sukkos Festival of Tabernacles
TANACH - Scriptures
TEFILLIN - phylacteries
TEHILLIM - Psalms
TZITZIS - fringes worn on a four cornered garment
TZORAAS - Leprosy
YAAKOV - Jacob
YECHEZKEL - Ezekiel
YEHOSHUA - Joshua
YERUSHALAYIM - Jerusalem
YESHAYAH - Isaiah
YIBBUM - levirate marriage where the wife of one who died without progeny, marries his brother
YIRMIYAH - Jeremiah
YISRAEL - Israel
YITZCHOK - Isaac
YOSEF - Joseph